MW00532188

Praise for
Feminine Emergence

Lisa has written a jaw-droppingly great book. *Feminine Emergence* bypasses the intellectual discourse on the differences between men and women, between masculine and feminine energies and offers up concise, inspired and clear solutions to how we can live an authentic and integrated life in service of our personal and professional success. It's not a self-help book or dry analytical study of the problem. It's a vibrant and alive call to arms that challenges the reader to turn inward, find their own answers and then dares them to live those answers in a loud and unapologetic way for the benefit of all. Read this book at your ego's risk. Your spirit and career will thank you.

— Michael C. Bryan, Founder, MCBHappier Coaching

Dr. Liszcz's book, *Feminine Emergence*, is honest storytelling that does not stop at her personal experience. She gives us a panoramic window to discover how our fellow women feel "in a man's world" and how we all can build more compassionate, integrated family and working relationships. What you will read will heal, educate and prepare you for current realities, but also for the future we all need to create.

— Celeste Sumoza, Psychologist, Development and Leadership Coach

With *Feminine Emergence*, Lisa M. Liszcz, Ph.D. has written an essential narrative for our time. This is a compelling story and relevant to all men and women working in the corporate world. Dr. Liszcz cuts through the BS and gets right to the heart of why and how women are treated differently, and she wisely offers a path for change.

— Teresa Duryea Wong, Former Corporate Executive; Current Joyful & Balanced Entrepreneur

Guys, don't be put off by the title! *Feminine Emergence* will help you understand the challenges women face in the workplace, how their male colleagues can make the business culture more inclusive, and how everyone can lead a more balanced life by embracing their feminine and masculine strengths. In a smooth, engaging narrative, behavioral scientist and career coach Dr. Lisa Liszcz shares her personal story, insights gained from her extensive work with women professionals, and practical suggestions for building successful careers in the #MeToo era.

— Ron Bitto, President, Bitto Marketing Consultants

Feminine Emergence is a great testament to never giving up and living life authentically. It is an excellent reminder of the past and a fresh perspective into what can be an energetic future.

— Kim Nugent Ed.D., Best selling author of Promotion Protocol

Many of the stories in *Feminine Emergence* parallel with experiences numerous have faced in the corporate world. Dr. Liszcz does an excellent job in conveying the emotions she encountered. Lisa's question, "What is your sphere of influence?" challenges us to reflect on where we are today in our efforts to BE THE CHANGE in ourselves or our workplace. I would recommend this book for anyone who is seeking personal and/or professional growth.

— Annella Metoyer, President, Inspire Development; Speaker, Author, and Coach

Feminine Emergence is a superb book that combines grit and exciting storytelling with compelling urgency to drive change. Dr. Lisa Liszcz gives a courageous and candid account of her personal journey inspiring all readers, regardless of background. Highly Recommended!

— Vera Verdree, Ph.D., Global Corporate Leader and Technology Expert

Lisa Liszcz has written a thought-provoking book that lays bare our culture's denigration of all things feminine — creativity, compassion, caring for self and others, etc. Drawing on her own experiences and those of her colleagues and clients, Dr. Liszcz examines the effect on businesses and personal lives of treating feminine traits as "less than" and challenges us to re-think societal norms and consider the extent to which each of us has adapted our lives to favor masculine over feminine energy and at what cost. She also provides useful tips for embracing feminine energy so that we can lead fuller and more joyful lives.

— Kathy Silver, Trial Lawyer focusing on Energy Litigation and Commercial Litigation Matters

It takes dedication to discover your truth. It takes courage to express it. Lisa Liszcz, Ph.D. in *Feminine Emergence*, has shown us she has both of these qualities. *Feminine Emergence* transcends gender. It's about becoming a true and whole human being. It's about having a richer, fuller and more meaningful life. *Feminine Emergence* is about balanced proportioning and integration of all aspects of your true Self. It's about living a life of integrity. If you're still evolving as a human being, read this book. If you've stopped evolving, read this book. If you never started, read this book! You'll be greatly rewarded.

— Graden Keller, Founder kellerconsulting™ Houston | New York City | London

Feminine Emergence (FE) is the epitome of creating profound shifts in our personal and professional lives. In this book, Dr. Lisa Liszcz courageously and confidently shares her vulnerability, anecdotal accounts, case studies, and investigations around the importance, intelligence and impact of our feminine energy in life. Despite the advancement, diversity, and openness in our society today, Lisa bravely exposes the extreme imbalance between the core foundation of our existence — the balancing act of masculine and feminine energies in our environments. This book showcases positive lessons from adversity through the harsh realities that most professionals face in their lives today. Lisa offers a powerful and purposeful path, along with practical steps to creating corporate cultures, organizations, and homes that are sensitive, whole and aligned with our true talents! She encourages us to identify and apply our innate gifts, intuitiveness, and feminine energy. Irrespective of our gender, we all can, should and must embrace the responsibility of creating harmonious and purposeful societies and organizations that are whole. I highly recommend reading this book to calm your ego, to open your heart and mind, and to allow your feminine power to emerge. Your soul will be grateful.

— Gagan Sarkaria, Soul, Branding & Money Coach | Branding Your Brilliance Expert | Founder & CEO of Unfold Your Success, LLC

Feminine Emergence™
Mindful Methods to Create Profound Shifts in Personal and Corporate Life
Copyright © 2018 by Lisa M. Liszcz, Ph.D.

ALL RIGHTS RESERVED. This book contains material protected under International and Federal Copyright Laws and Treaties. Any unauthorized reprint or use of this material is prohibited. No part of this book may be reproduced or transmitted in any form or by any means, electronic or mechanical, including photocopying, recording, or by any information storage and retrieval system without the written permission from the author/publisher.

Publisher: Tom Bird Retreats, Inc.
For Penny Publishing, a Division of Liszcz Consulting, LLC.
Paperback ISBN: 978-1-62747-326-2
Hardcover ISBN: 978-1-62747-327-9
Ebook ISBN: 978-1-62747-328-6

Contact Lisa M. Liszcz, Ph.D. at:
Email: Lisa@LisaLiszcz.com
Web: LisaLiszcz.com | FeminineEmergence.love

Credits:
Cover Designers: Gagan Sarkaria, M.F.A, M.B.A, & Abbey Wilkerson, B.F.A.
UnfoldYourSuccess.com
Interior Layout & Design: Gagan Sarkaria & Abbey Wilkerson
Book Cover Sales Copy & Content Editing: Gagan Sarkaria
Author Photo: Tonya Dailey

Feminine Emergence Complete Branding, Art Direction, Design & Production:
Gagan Sarkaria & Abbey Wilkerson

Feminine Emergence

Lisa M. Liszcz, Ph.D.

Dedication

This book is dedicated to all girls, boys, women, and men who have ever shunned or stifled their feminine energy.

May you learn to embrace your gifts from the divine feminine.

I hope you skip and dance whenever you want, live your life with compassion, emotion and flair, and you are always in tune with your intuition.

You are our future.

Acknowledgements

It is with great pleasure that I share my thoughts, research, and recommendations on feminine emergence with you. I'm excited about changes in our culture and the emergence of feminine energy. I enjoyed exploring this phenomenon and next steps to write this book.

Besides personal accounts and accounts from my clients and research, I've included stories from headlines and popular culture as evidence. In most cases, I've changed names and personal information to preserve anonymity of those to whom I refer. A number of exchanges described are re-created from memory, and I have recalled and written about them to the best of my ability.

Thanks to everyone who gave me input, feedback and support during the writing of this book. Thank you to all the women I interviewed during 2016 and to men and women who shared their stories with me and trusted me to use their stories to make a positive difference in this world.

Personally, I give special thanks to Liz Sampson, Kathy Silver, Marcy Brazaitis, Donna Turner, Joanie Patrick, Teresa Wong, Maggie May Hammock, Kim Nugent, and Celeste Sumoza for cheering me on. Your encouragement has meant the world to me. Thanks to John Hodgkinson, and Tom Bird for showing me the ropes as a new author. Thank you to Michael C. Bryan for getting me started on this process, reading my first pages, and telling me that I could and needed to write a book. You told me that writing a book would change me, and it did. Thank you to Gagan Sarkaria for midwifing me through the very final stages of birthing this baby and for your amazing and inspired design work on the cover and throughout the book. You are truly extraordinary! And thank you so much to Ron Bitto, Graden Keller, Vera Verdree, Annella Metoyer, Celeste Sumoza, Teresa Wong, Kathy Silver, Michael C. Bryan, Janet William, and Karen Collyer for reading my manuscript and giving me feedback. You're all such kind and generous souls!

Most of all and with my entire heart that is so full of gratitude, thank you to my amazing and wonderful husband, Michael Link. Without you this book would not have been possible. Dear, you are my rock and my love. You are one of the most masculine/feminine energy balanced people I know, and I admire and adore you completely. Thank you for your support and for believing in me. I love you so very, very much.

Prologue

My divorce was one of the most dark and yet liberating periods of my life. I felt rejected, worthless, alone, crushed, and thought all my dreams had died. As I embarked on a new life, I slowly began my transformation into the woman I was born to be. One step at a time, I aligned with my purpose and found joy. It was a long, slow process with twists and turns, stops and starts as I journeyed from pain to purpose.

I came across a reading about dragonflies surviving on our planet for over 300 million years. I learned that dragonflies are ancient symbols of change, perseverance, lightness of being, poise, and courage. Female dragonflies lay their eggs in small water bodies such as ponds. Aquatic larvae hatch from eggs. The aquatic larvae are called "nymphs". The nymphs may live up to 4 years before transforming into adult dragonflies and may shed their skin up to 17 times (LearnAboutNature.com 2018). Reading about how long dragonflies have been on the planet and how much change dragonflies endure gave me encouragement.

I fell in love with dragonflies and what they symbolize. With the help of my beautiful, loving stepmother, Phyllis, I filled my new home with dragonflies on kitchen towels, trivets, paper weights, mugs and yard art. Even my shower curtain had dragonflies embroidered on it. I wore clothes and jewelry adorned with dragonflies. Everywhere I looked I was reminded that I too could persevere, be courageous, open myself up to transformation, and embrace lightness. Dragonflies lifted me in my dark days and inspired me to be tenacious. I transformed my pain into a new life.

Change comes slowly. Change for individuals and cultures happens step by step, one instance at a time. Sometimes we think change is not happening because we cannot see it in our daily lives. The nymph does not know she will become the dragonfly. Her job is to persevere with courage and poise.

Embrace the dragonfly, my friends. Persevere. Be courageous and light. Our world is transforming. Let's be the change and be courageous together.

> "

DRAGONFLIES HAVE BEEN ON OUR PLANET FOR
OVER 300 MILLION YEARS. WHEN YOU BELIEVE YOU
MAY FALTER, REMEMBER THE DRAGONFLY.
PERSEVERE. HAVE COURAGE. EMBRACE LIGHTNESS.
—Lisa Liszcz

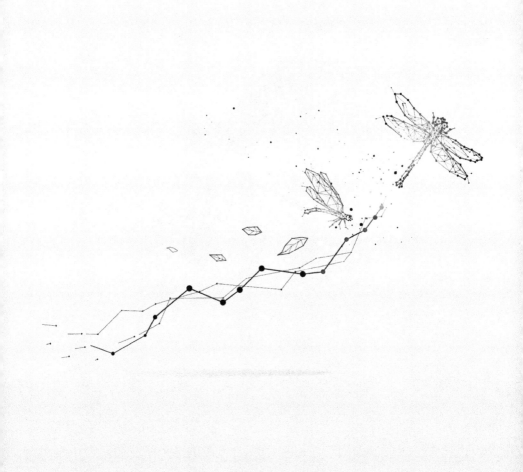

Table of Contents

Peripheral

CHAPTER 1

ON THE SIDELINES

When I watch sports, I feel for the players on the bench. They want to be in the game. They want to play. The coaches (many are former players) have high blood pressure and high heart rates during games, often higher than those of the players on the court or field. Players in the game can contribute to and impact the game's result. The players are in their flow, doing what they were trained and love to do.

Business professionals are like sports professionals, they don't want to sit on the sideline. If they've invested in a career and a profession they love, excel at and feel committed to, they want to be "in the game." They feel exhilarated and purposeful when they are contributing to desired outcomes.

Too many professionals today still get sidelined. They do not adequately take part in professional teams, executive teams, and boards. They are not contributing fully, instead they run on the periphery. Players who are in the game keep non-players "on the bench" and only tap others like themselves to play for any real minutes and big plays.

What is the game that business professionals play? This game is "Corporate America." White men are on the court. On the bench are men of color, women, people in the LGBTQ community, immigrants, and others who are not mainstream. We've made improvements since the civil rights era and since implementing the

Equal Employment Opportunity Commission. I'm proud of those improvements, but we have more to do. I entered the workforce as a professional in 1986 and was shocked at how many challenges existed. I saw harassment, discrimination, and cliques affecting productivity and work quality. Today, I'm surprised at how slow we are to make improvements in our work cultures.

After the growth of the #MeToo and #TimesUp movements in the entertainment industry in 2017, I reflected on my experiences and those of women I know working in American business offices. I thought of where we've made progress in our corporate cultures in the last thirty years, where we have more opportunities, and what methods we can use to make improvements. I speculated on how to speed up change and integration of everyone's talents in the next thirty years. I understand our country's productivity and competitiveness depends on engaging all our talent. The United States can use its business offices to show the world that the great melting pot experiment works, and that we are a respectful nation.

My feminist sensibilities began in college and graduate school in the 1980s. In the late 1990s, I was working for a manufacturing company in a rural community and taking classes towards my Ph.D. at night at a city college. I had lost none of my passion for the rights of women, minorities and other protected groups. Working in the "real world" made them grow. Something as simple as a poster on the wall that I thought was insensitive could agitate me.

THAT DAMN POSTER

I hated that poster. Every night when I passed it going to and from class, I felt it was mocking me. I was determined to make that poster a lie. There was a woman on it. If there is a classic image of what a professional woman should look like, this was her. She was wearing a dark suit, she had her hair up, and she was in an office working on papers. The poster hung in the building on campus where most of my Ph.D. classes were at the University of Houston. It was a huge poster, like a movie poster in a theater, so, it was hard to miss. The poster had a printed summary of a research article on it, which was long and in small print. The picture of the woman was huge.

I walked up to the poster one day to see what the hell it was about. It didn't look like something you'd see at the college campus. The images I saw on the walls around campus were of the university, downtown Houston, or student activities. The research article reported that many women left their jobs to be entrepreneurs because they did not like the environment at their companies.

The poster is long gone (I saw it in the late 1990s), but the gist of what it said was that increasingly, women experienced frustration in male-dominated, hierarchical environments of medium and large-sized companies. They felt they did not experience independence and the creative opportunities they wanted and needed to achieve success. They felt held back and stifled. I thought that was a strange poster to put on the wall at the University of Houston, it was an odd message to promote. It seemed negative. I felt angry and disappointed.
I thought to myself, "That'll never happen to me. I will stay the course."

I thought that my personal and professional satisfaction could be achieved by growing my career at a large company. I worked as a mid-level manager at a manufacturing company. The work was not that difficult, and I made a good income. I liked the prestige of being at a company with name recognition - a global company with a long history. The poster pissed me off. Maybe deep down, I knew there was a part of me that the poster described. Maybe all those years ago, I knew there was truth in what it said. As they say, the truth hurts.

I was working full time during the day and taking classes at night. Between home, work, and school, I drove over 100 miles a day, often eating at least one meal in my car while driving, trying to not spill anything on myself. I studied, researched and wrote papers on the weekends. I also had a husband, owned a home and had two stepchildren. My plate was full.

On Friday nights I collapsed from exhaustion, but I felt good about everything I was doing, so I kept going. It felt like a badge of honor to be doing so much, to have so much on my plate. For years, I had to walk by that damn poster that I hated on my way to class, and again on my way from class. Every time I saw that poster, I felt like it was mocking me and all professional women... telling us, we couldn't "hack it," that we couldn't take the heat, couldn't do the work. It interpreted entrepreneurship as an easier path than working in a corporate environment. I felt like the poster was saying, "Women take the easier path." It pissed me off, and I became more determined to attain success in the corporate environment I was working in.

I have been successful by many measures in corporate America. Many women have been. It's difficult, and I'm not sure if it's gotten easier over the last twenty-five years. Women are not looking for an easy experience. Women, like men, want challenges at work, just not the kinds of challenges that have no real meaning. Men and women I've coached want challenging, meaningful work. Women do not enjoy challenges like defending their ability to do a job that they're qualified to do, or defending themselves against a variety of types of harassment, or explaining that they're not little girls or crazy, and do in fact know how to make and execute decisions. Women enjoy challenges that are about work, not challenges that are about their gender.

For over twenty-five years I've coached professionals, including many women. I've spent my career in a variety of industries that were all male-dominated. I've worked in Houston, a city I love and that has elements of grittiness and machismo that permeate corporate cultures, and I've worked for European and American companies. They all had similarities and differences. There were pros and cons to each.

I have coached hundreds of professional women on what it's like to work in these environments. Last year, I worked on a project that fascinated me — I conducted one-on-one interviews with forty-four mid-career women. I asked them about their careers, what they are most proud of, what (if given a chance) they would have done differently, and how happy they are now in their careers.

I found that many women in their forties and fifties have frustrations, and they have had experiences that they are proud of, and they have valuable insights to share. For many of us, the road has taken unexpected twists and turns, and there have certainly been surprises. They've had experiences no one should have, and they've mostly kept quiet about them. So have I.

I am an entrepreneur now. I did not plan this career trajectory. A week before my 50th birthday, I was laid off. It turned out to be a blessing. I was out of balance and needed to restore a healthy balance to my life and take my career in a new direction. Like the women I interviewed, I had become exhausted and burned out. I was proud of what I had accomplished, now I wanted to focus on what was next for me and what would bring me joy. I spent a lot of time in introspection, and I found parallels to my journey in changes in our U.S. culture during the last decade. As I evolved, I saw our country evolve too.

That damn poster was right. Now I understand why. I am glad I noticed it and looked at it. I've experienced the story written on the poster, and my version is too big for a poster.

I'm not alone. Many people share this story, and I want to share what I learned with you.

BRA STRAPS

I started my professional career in 1986 when I graduated from college and landed my first professional position. I was thrilled. I had heard women and minorities still had challenges in the workforce and I learned about discrimination and harassment in school. I thought I was prepared for challenges and promised myself I would succeed. I admired women in the media like Barbara Walters and Oprah Winfrey. I grew up watching Mary Tyler Moore on TV, and now I watched Murphy Brown.

Nothing prepared me for how chauvinistic the workforce still was. I began working at a manufacturing site in a rural area outside of Houston, Texas, a few months after graduating from college. Some employees there provided a steady diet of sexual innuendos, teasing and touching. Women and men participated; men participated more. Glenn, an older man and senior executive, was one of the worst. Before I give you an example, I'll give you some background.

In this environment, we often got work done in casual side conversations before and after meetings and in hallways. We could catch somebody to answer a quick question or to get a signature. It was part of the culture. I worked for Kathy. Kathy's boss's boss, Glenn, fancied himself quite the ladies' man. He often touched, touching your arm, putting his arm around you or standing so close beside you that his arm touched yours. He only did this with women, attractive younger women. He would give women shoulder massages, and (for some reason, I will never understand) he would rub the bra strap on your back through your blouse.

One day, Kathy and I were talking with her boss, John, in the hallway. We were discussing getting budget approval for engineering work to renovate a building. Glenn walked up, snuggled up to Kathy with one hand on her shoulder and the other hand rubbing her bra strap, and asked, "What are we talking about?"

Kathy's and my eyes met. I thought she would hurl. My stomach contracted, and I quit breathing for a few seconds. When you're young, as we were, there's nothing like seeing a fat man who is old enough to be your dad and so cocksure of himself touching your friend to make you want to lose your lunch, except maybe if he touches you. I wanted to say, "Keep your hands to yourself, you sick bastard!" but I didn't. We both just wrapped up the conversation and moved on.

One insidious aspect of harassment is that it is difficult to speak up at the time. The purpose of harassment is to make you feel weak. Victims want it to stop. We try to move on, bury it, and hope to God, the Universe, or whatever that it will never happen again. I've interviewed over a hundred women in the past twenty-five years about harassment. At that moment, feelings of shame and disgust arise and mix with shock and astonishment. Women swallow these feelings, push them down and ignore them. We try to operate on top of them. The feelings move into our unconscious and our bodies, and they hide there — under the surface.

Neither Kathy nor I were in a position to protest or correct Glenn. We needed and liked our jobs; we liked the work and most of our colleagues. Glenn had friends and colleagues who would stand up for him in the organization. Plus, to many, what Glenn did probably seemed harmless and "friendly." I am still convinced that it was intended to demean Kathy and to keep us in our place. He sent the message, "Don't get too big for your britches, little lady. Remember who's in charge around here."

As an executive, Glenn wielded substantial power in the organization. He used touching, harassment and bullying to remind people of the pecking order. To invade personal space is disrespectful. Touching another person without permission is ignorant. Doing that to someone who you know is not in a position to stand up for themselves is bullying, and it's wrong.

Upon greeting, men shook hands or slapped on the back. With women, men inappropriately touched, invaded personal space, gave shoulder massages, teased and flirted. Women wanted to build relationships. We also wanted to be respected as professionals. Hiring professional women at plant sites was still new. Men often thought of women colleagues as women, not as professionals. Some men objectified women colleagues. It surprised me how often this happened.

PARTY GIRLS

Frequently, executives would invite Kathy and me to dinner meetings. One day Kathy asked me, "You know why we get invited to those dinner meetings, right?" I thought Kathy and I were working on important projects and that executives in our company wanted to hear about our projects and get to know us professionally. I also thought that Kathy and I added value to the meetings with information and insights. Clearly, mentors were watching out for us and were helping us to build our professional networks. There seemed to me to be a plethora of valid reasons for us to be invited to dinner meetings. But I was naïve. I didn't answer Kathy. I started to feel confused. I knew I was missing something.

Kathy said, "It's because we're fun, and they think we're 'party girls.'" When the big cheeses didn't want to go all out and take dignitaries to strip clubs, they invited the "party girls" to the dinner. She explained that she thought we were invited when the managers didn't want to spring for professional dancers.

Damn, that pissed me off. I thought I was there because I was bright and had high potential. After that, we got very selective about which dinners we went to. We only went if we felt there were strategic advantages for us, and we were always very professional, extra professional. We were smart and savvy. I think about this story and the stories that I hear from my clients. This story could have happened to me thirty years ago, twenty, ten, or five.

When I joined the workforce in 1986, I was one of about five professional women out of about 800 employees where I worked. The idea of a "professional woman" was novel. The work location was miles wide and miles long like a large college campus or Disney World. It was not Disney World. There were at least twelve different buildings at the site. Some of them only had men's restrooms, no restrooms for women. They had been built that way years before.

Any organization that is just starting to integrate women professionals or women leaders has a lot of work to do to manage change. That was true then, and it's true now. The existing population simply does not know what to expect or what is expected of them. When you can import someone with knowledge and experience to help the transition, this can accelerate the success of the entire workforce. Otherwise, transition moves more slowly.

ARE YOU CRAZY?

One example of change taking a long time, longer than necessary, includes our double standards. We still have double standards in the workforce. We judge and label women as bitchy, aggressive, and crazy or hormonal, when we call men strong, powerful and innovative.

When women break new ground others whisper, "Who does she think she is?" or, "Good Lord, what is she up to now?" The image of the moody, emotional, or hysterical woman perseveres (Little 2015). I experienced this once when my boss's boss and a group of other male leaders called me a "crazy lady" for creating solutions to challenging training problems. I learned that when a woman acts, she is "crazy."

Our company needed to hire more employees than we had ever hired. We were growing by leaps and bounds, and needed talent to support our growth. We planned to hire ten times more employees during one calendar year than we had ever hired before in a single year. Our training rooms were too small to fit the large groups of new employees we would put through orientations and "new employee" training programs. As head of the training department, I was responsible for solving this problem.

After consulting with team members, I decided to convert smaller rooms into larger rooms so that trainers could speak to larger groups of fifty people at a time instead of just twenty or thirty. This way we moved new employees through their training in half the time and with fewer trainers. I called a design expert in our Engineering and Architecture group. He said we could take a few non-load-bearing walls out and make nice, big classrooms. I approved the work, and they got started. The rooms turned out beautifully. By leveraging our small group of trainers and other limited resources with the large training rooms, we trained large groups of new employees and met our goals.

My boss's boss said to me one day when the construction was being done, "I'm defending your behaviors to the other men on the leadership team." He chuckled. I asked why.

"They are asking me what the 'crazy lady' in training is doing knocking out all the walls in the training department. They're saying you've lost your mind."

I thanked him for his support. Maybe he was embarrassed about having to "defend" me. I don't know. It makes sense that instead of the men on the leadership team assuming I'd made a strategic decision to support company goals, they assumed that the woman running the training department had lost her mind. Their reaction was disrespectful. They would have praised a man for being "bold" and "action-oriented." Not a woman. I knew this was unfair, but also normal. For the environment, the interpretation was normal. I was used to this style of reaction because of the way my parents raised me. More on that later.

This happened twenty years ago. I would like to think workplace cultures and our societal culture have become more supportive of professional women and women in leadership. I'd like to say we have made noteworthy progress. But, we continue to fight an uphill battle. Change is slow. Women have worked as professionals for generations. Changes have occurred, but we need to stay ever-vigilant to continue to make progress for women and other protected groups in the workplace.

The goal is that everyone gets the respect they deserve. For each individual to be able to contribute their talents and skills, they need to feel safe, supported and respected. For companies to succeed and compete, we need everyone's talents and skills. We need people to succeed so that businesses can succeed.

The success of business cannot be separated from the success of people, all people — men and women.

66

WE SUPPORT DOUBLE-STANDARDS IN THE WORKPLACES.
TO BE SUCCESSFUL ALL EMPLOYEES
MUST FEEL SAFE AND RESPECTED.
—Lisa Liszcz

2

Indispensable

CHAPTER 2

WOMEN WORKING — IN HISTORY

Women work in the arts, sciences, business, medicine, politics and more. We've made contributions and provided inspiration and role modeling in these areas for generations. Women have invented, led, and broken new ground, reminding us of the important role women have had not only in the home but also at work. Often, these women are not written about in history books. We don't learn about them, so we don't know about them. Remembering great inventors and scientists as men supports gender stereotypes which leave women on an unequal footing in our society.

As creatives, women advanced the world of inventing. Mary Anderson invented the windshield wiper and earned the patent for a swinging arm with a rubber blade in 1903. By 1913, the windshield wiper became standard equipment on cars.

Rosalyn Yalow invented radioimmunoassay, the equipment needed for analyzing minute substances in urine and blood such as hormones.

Stephanie Kwolek invented Kevlar®, which is invaluable in dozens of applications including bulletproof vests, safety helmets, and suspension bridge cables.

Grace Murray Hopper, Ph.D. pioneered computer programming, popularizing the idea of machine-independent programming languages which led to the development of COBOL, an early, user-friendly programming language (Beyer 2009). You can find and watch an interview Grace did with David Letterman if you Google "Grace Hopper and Letterman." It's a delightful interview.

Many of us learned about Dorothy Vaughan, Mary Jackson, Katherine Johnson and Christine Darden from the 2016 movie, *Hidden Figures*. These four African American women participated in some of NASA's greatest successes in science, mathematics and engineering (Shetterly 2016).

Reading about modern-day women inventors and their contributions is fascinating. I got no exposure to these women in school. I don't remember reading about women making major contributions to science and innovation. For more information, see the website Famous Women Inventors at women-inventors.com. Women contributed for generations in science. But on the flip side, how many were held back or not allowed for "being a girl?" And what were the costs to those individuals, their families, and our society in lost potential and lost discoveries? More on this in Chapter 3. In our parents' and grandparents' generations, women inventors and scientists represented anomalies more than norms. People thought of them as unusual, or even strange. Today, we have more women and girls working in science, technology, engineering, and math, but how many are held back?

Women excelled in business for generations. Anna Bissell became CEO of the Bissell sweeper company in 1889 with great success (Worthen 2016). In 1972, Katharine Graham became America's first female CEO of a Fortune 500 Company when she became CEO of The Washington Post, and for over two decades, she built a publishing empire (Worthen 2016). Many of us learned about Katharine in the movie, *The Post*.

Ursula Burns became the first African American Woman CEO of a Fortune 500 Company when she succeeded Anne Mulcahy in that position at Xerox in 2009 (Worthen 2016). Ursula went on to lead the White House National STEM program and serve in many other notable roles (2018). Many of our top business leaders today are women (Bellstrom and Kowitt 2017).

Women today don't just lead human resource or healthcare businesses (traditional areas for women), we lead manufacturing and technology companies like General Motors and Lockheed Martin. In 2017, twenty-six women CEOs led companies controlling more than $1.1 trillion in market capitalization (Bellstrom and Kowitt 2017). And for wildly successful entrepreneurs, look no further than Yang Lan (cofounder of Sun Media), Arianna Huffington (founder of Huffington Post), Weili Dai (cofounder of Marvell Technologies), and Sara Blakely (the Founder of Spanx, Inc.) (Casserly 2018).

We find women in key leadership positions often, but not as often as our education and job entry level numbers predict. Compared to men, women leaders in business are few. Women go to college and land jobs, but we do not get promoted at an equal rate to men. I'll discuss this later in this chapter.

Women challenge rules, chart new territories, and - yes - break glass ceilings. Women "firsts" happen regularly. They happen everyday on large and small stages. Some of our big stage "firsts" include Hillary Rodham Clinton being the first woman nominated to a major political party's candidacy for President, Madeleine Albright serving as our first woman U.S. Secretary of State, and Alice Waters, the first woman to win the prestigious James Beard Award for Outstanding Chef (2017). Politics and culinary arts are classic "boys' clubs." When women make progress in these clubs, we are breaking thick, solid glass ceilings.

One of my favorite stories from Time Magazine's landmark issue on women firsts, released in September 2017, is about Jennifer Yuh Nelson (2017). Jennifer solo-directed a major Hollywood animated feature, *Kung Fu Panda*. Her producer, Melissa Cobb, eased Jennifer into the director role by gradually showing her she had the skills to do the job, sometimes being a bit tricky. When asked to direct, Jennifer said, "No, no. I'm too quiet; I'm too introverted." Melissa reminded Jennifer that she had already directed a scene that had come out well, and that she had enjoyed doing it.

Melissa set up that introduction to directing to prove to Jennifer that she had what it takes, and to build her confidence in time for the next movie direction opportunity. I love this story because it shows one woman believing in another and playing a vital role in mentoring and encouraging a more junior woman professional in the male-dominated field of entertainment.

WOMEN IN COLLEGE, WORK AND LEADERSHIP

I come across stories like this regularly. I read about a new CEO of a household-name company, and it's a woman. I read about an invention or scientific breakthrough, and the team leader is a woman. I hear on the radio about a global company starting an initiative on "Women in Leadership." These are great stories. They inspire and motivate, making me feel like we are making progress, and I get excited. However, big change comes with big numbers. A "token promotion" here and a "woman team leader" there will not change corporate culture.

Tokens are not change agents. Once, I served on a leadership team for three years. I was the only woman and I held the lowest level job on the team. The team worked dysfunctionally when I arrived and when I left. My boss told me, "I thought you would change them." I had no leverage and no authority. We needed a longer time to change a team with such a dysfunctional history. It takes a critical mass of aligned individuals to change culture. It takes a tipping point. I will cover more on this in Chapter 7.

Corporate cultures changed in the last thirty years, just not as much as we hoped they would. In corporations today, professional women are not novel, yet we don't have equal numbers to men in leadership roles. Why is this? Thirty years ago, 48% of graduates with business degrees were women (Digest of Education Statistics 2016). Where are these women? What happened to them? Perhaps they dropped out like "that damn poster" explained. Perhaps they are still in the workforce, but they are not seen as "leadership material" or don't want to be in leadership roles.

Companies hired women over the last thirty years but did not engage, promote and retain them enough to get them into leadership roles. Professional women may have expected more than companies offered: fairness, respect, support. Women would have benefited if corporate cultures embraced their unique strengths.

That did not happen. Companies recruited women and then expected them to fit in and become little men - the women needed to change. The companies did not change, and failed to integrate and leverage the unique strengths that women brought.

I spent ten years of my career working inside corporations as a professional in talent management; this gave me the chance to have career discussions with hundreds of professionals working in global companies. I continue this work in my coaching practice now. These professionals are bright men and women in their twenties and thirties, fully focused on their careers. They express ambition, willingness to travel and work internationally, and a strong desire to learn and be challenged. I find it inspiring to work with these talented professionals and to hear their stories and goals. I enjoy coaching them about how to move forward in their careers and helping make promotions possible for them.

As I have career discussions, the topic of family and children comes up. I talk with all the professionals I coach about family and children, it does not matter if they were men or women. I discuss career and work-life balance with both men and women, but it is a different conversation. Men and women share that their roles in raising children, caring for aging parents and taking care of the home differ. Differences in home and family responsibilities are well documented (Labor 2017), with women taking on more responsibility for caring for the home and family members.

It can become a career issue from the company's perspective regarding promotability when a woman has or plans to have children, or to care for parents. Leaders see her as less mobile. Maybe she wouldn't be able to travel as much for business, or maybe she would be less willing to work internationally. Leaders don't discuss family impact on men as often, with men seen as free to pursue their careers without limitations imposed by family or children. I have seen a few cases in the last five to ten years where executive women hire nannies, or their husbands stay home to raise children, and the executive woman has the freedom to enjoy a family and a full, challenging career at a president or C-suite level. I've spoken with two of these women one-on-one about their experiences. I will talk more about what they shared with me in Chapter 9.

Today, more women join the workforce than ever before. In the U.S. 56.8% of women aged sixteen years and above were in the labor force in 2016, 61.5% of mothers with children under the age of three were in the labor force, and women held 51.5% of combined management and professional positions during 2016 (Catalyst 2017). More women enter and graduate from college and graduate schools than ever before, and more women enter the workforce as professionals than ever before according to the United States Department of Labor (Labor 2017).

In fact, women earn more bachelors and graduate degrees than men in the United States. Women earn 25% more bachelor's degrees than men, 32% more masters degrees than men, and 9% more doctoral degrees than men in the United States (Digest of Education Statistics 2016). In many professions that require degrees, the number of women entering the workforce is equal to the number of men or higher. In general, women are slightly more likely to be hired after graduation from college, but men are paid more (Adams 2015). There is an exception among one group. Among Millennials, women are getting hired and paid more (Pianin 2017) coming out of college.

In many professions, the number of women entering the workforce is equal to the number of men or higher. Differences in gender ratios begin as people are promoted into management. Then we start to see more men than women. From management, up to the executive level and into the boardroom, the proportion of women decreases. In 2016, women made up only 20.2% of all board seats of Fortune 500 companies in the United States (Catalyst 2017). Since women control 80% of consumer spending in the United States, companies would benefit by promoting more women to leadership positions.

It is time for women to be seen as equals and to realize equal opportunities and support in the workplace. It does not matter if that workplace is in entertainment, education, medicine, politics, business, or another profession. Now is the time for fairness and respect for women in all industries. Integration and inclusion will make businesses stronger and more competitive and allow for everyone to realize their potential and share their gifts.

Researchers confirm that "teams with an equal gender mix perform better than male-dominated teams in terms of sales and profits" (Boatman 2011; Hoogendoorn, Oosterbeek, and van Praag 2013). Preservation of a male-dominated workforce is a shot in the foot. Where women lead companies, employees rate those companies higher on leadership, and the sales and profits are higher. Promoting larger numbers of women into senior positions in companies benefits companies in their culture and at their bottom lines.

WHY ARE WE STILL NOT LEADERS?

In companies and as entrepreneurs, women are successful. There is no doubt about women's ability and interest in doing high-level work. Women create success for themselves and others. We sit in the corner office and the boardroom, but our numbers are few and we often feel isolated. We work creatively, independently, collaboratively, and analytically.

So, why do we still have such low numbers of women in senior leadership in companies? Clearly, women have contributed for generations. Women are getting educated and getting jobs. Women earned almost half of the business degrees thirty years ago. Why do we have this persistent absence of women at the top? There are several reasons, and it's a complex issue. Who's to blame? Well, we all are — men and women. Men and women still question the ability of women to lead and contribute.

Yes, we women even question ourselves.

My goal is to explain why this happens and suggest solutions that everyone can engage in for the benefit of our own lives and for the companies we support.

I hear men talk about concerns of losing power.

There will be no loss of power.

There will only be gains in power as power grows and is shared and spread. Look around. Power, energy, abundance, and affluence grow like muscadine vines in the Texas summer heat. There is no stopping it. We will enjoy positive, constructive competition and action orientation together. These energies will be balanced with creativity, collaboration and nurturing. Right now, organizations are fundamentally missing out on half of what is naturally provided in our world, half of the energy and benefits.

When U.S. businesses become more energized and more productive, there will be additional positive power for everyone to leverage. There is nothing lost, there is only gain. There is more for all of us. More to enjoy. More abundance.

The changes will not happen overnight. Like all large transformations, this transformation will be gradual but with building momentum. It needs to keep moving. To have a hand in the next positive step for our country and our world is a tremendous honor that I anticipate many leaders and non-leaders will embrace once they see the benefits for themselves and others.

"

ABUNDANCE GROWS FOR ALL WHEN WE
LEVERAGE EVERYONE'S GIFTS.
WITH GROWTH, POWER EXPANDS.
—Lisa Liszcz

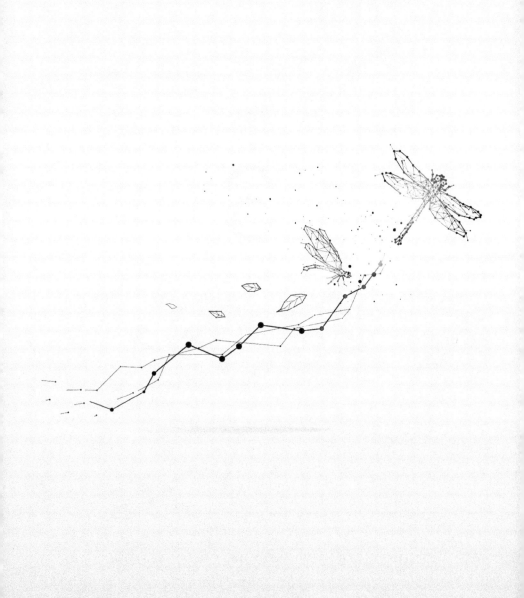

3

The Mainstream and The Other

CHAPTER 3

KEEPING WOMEN OUT OF THE CLUB

Throughout my corporate career, I regularly dealt with misogynistic bullying or harassment. Most of the women and some men I coach also report dealing with bullying and harassment. It seems to be part of many business and professional cultures. Some environments were better than others, but there is at least some low-level approval of harassing women at even the best companies and the shiniest corporate offices.

In every year of my career, in every work environment, corporate office, region office, or field office, I either directly experienced, observed or heard about harassment or assault. Most of the women I interviewed, and my women clients, have told me the same.

Harassment and assault are power behaviors. Perpetrators fill their need for dominance and control by harassing or assaulting their victims (Yonack 2018). However subtle or unconscious his behavior (most harassers are men) (Yonack), the perpetrator does what he does to keep his victim in "her place." He may do this with behaviors as subtle as a look or as egregious as assault, or using any behavior in between.

Egregious cases, the more shocking ones, get into the news. More subtle, non-grabby, non-touchy methods of harassment are more common and chip away at their target's self-esteem and productivity. They undermine a woman's ability to be the great leader she can be and keep her out of the "in-group" of power. Let me give you a few examples.

NON-GRABBY HARASSMENT IS STILL HARASSMENT

One woman executive told me that before she was hired at one of her last jobs, during the interview process she was asked by the COO (Chief Operating Officer) of the company, "You are not going to sue us, are you? Because, you know, women sue companies."

Imagine that you're close to landing a job at a company that pays well and has good benefits. You're trying to feed and provide for your family, and it's a tough job market. Jobs are hard to find. You are a talented expert in your field with excellent experience, as this woman was. Then you're asked that question. It is 100% inappropriate and demeaning. This question, however subtle, sends a clear message that says, "I don't trust you, and I wish I didn't have to hire you."

In a different job market, where many jobs are available, this woman may have answered differently. She said, "No, I am not going to sue you." She was mistreated at that company and was eventually laid off after a horrible experience in a misogynistic culture. The COO tipped his hand on the company's culture from the beginning, and she walked right into a bad situation.

One male executive I worked for was an especially bold harasser, and had a reputation for philandering with staff. He and I were working on databases in his office one evening, and were talking about how the databases needed to be configured to capture the data that we needed for our reports. We were reviewing data on six or seven different levels including, for example, Sr. Director, Director, Sr. Manager, Manager, Supervisor, and Employee. We discussed how many employee levels we should include in the reports, how many levels up and how many levels down.

He was behind his desk looking at the database on his computer, and I was sitting in the guest chair in front of his desk facing him. Suddenly, he turned his body to face me squarely, looked me in the eye, and said, "Why don't you tell me how far you like to go down?"

He smirked.

I was shocked.

I gave him my best, "Go fuck yourself," look, then got up and left his office. Like most of the women I talk with and coach, when something like this happens it is completely shocking, too shocking to be able to form words. Your brain goes to, "Did that really just happen? Damn!" because to most women, it is unbelievable. At that time, I could not articulate my thoughts when an inexcusable comment like that was targeted at me.

I've been harassed many times at work, and talked with many women who have also been harassed sexually and otherwise. I've investigated claims of sexual harassment for companies I've worked for as an HR professional, and I've heard everything from, "He keeps asking me out on a date, and I keep telling him 'No,'" to, "He walks up behind me and tells me, 'I want to put my penis in your vagina.'"

I've also personally been told by a man, "You know you've taken a job away from a man who needs to support a family, don't you?" and have talked with women who have been told similar things or been otherwise harassed. I'm not seeing significant signs of improvement. I hear a lot about continued frustration with pervasive inequities and lack of respect for women in the workplace. And women remain hesitant to speak up.

Men harass women to keep women from feeling empowered — empowered to speak up, make suggestions, lean in, ask for more, and insist on being heard. Men also harass women to keep women from feeling entitled — entitled to amazing careers, promotion and raise opportunities, and equal pay. This behavior can be partially conscious and partially unconscious. Unconsciously, both parties go to behavior that they've learned will maintain the status quo and balance of power in the company's culture. Consciously, they both know it is unlikely that a male executive will suffer major consequences. It is more likely that the woman will face negative consequences if she says something.

WHY WOMEN DON'T COMPLAIN

Usually, a harasser is in a senior position to his victim. When a woman stands up to a harasser, she will likely pay a price. He is likely to retaliate by giving her bad work assignments, a bad review, ostracizing her from the group, or in general making life hell for her. The company I worked for when my boss's boss asked me about "going down" was a company that had layoffs regularly, and I needed my job. I was looking for another job, but I wanted to leave on my own terms. I let it go. That's what most women tell me they do.

Women typically don't talk back; we don't stand up for ourselves or argue about a situation. When we are degraded, we let it go, hoping the behavior will stop on its own. We worry about it, and it wears at us, chipping away our self-esteem, just as it's intended to do - consciously or unconsciously. It sets in motion or propels an insidious cancer of self-questioning for so many of us. Women are usually the targets of sexual harassment (Yonack 2018), but it happens to men too and they suffer in the same ways when they are victims.

Few people talk about harassment, assault, inappropriate jokes, innuendos, or any of these behaviors in the workplace. That's just "the way it is." If we do talk about it, we joke about it. I've seen people get a bad reputation for whistle-blowing on this type of behavior. It is flat wrong that women or men would be labeled negatively for being whistle-blowers. Companies and leaders who are committed to high standards of conduct should want employees who don't tolerate harassment and discrimination. Talented professionals who are willing to speak up should be in high demand. It is not so. Everyone is supposed to "protect the company" and its executives. We have gotten to a point where in many corporate cultures following standard practices of good conduct, and the law (there are laws against harassment), is perceived as not being on the side of the company. It's not perceived as being part of the "in-group."

DON'T CALL ME "GIRL"

In addition to sexual harassment, I've seen women treated like little girls and imbeciles, which is infuriating and another way to limit our progress. One time I was approached about an internal promotion. The vice president, a man, came to me and talked about traveling extensively in the new role. I traveled extensively in previous jobs, but he did not know that as he did not take the time to check or ask me about my background.

He talked to me about the new internal opportunity. He said I would work for him and that we would be traveling globally together to facilitate focus groups on leadership development and to conduct research and classes for our company. He told me that before I accepted the opportunity I needed to check with "whoever I needed to check with" to make sure that was going to be okay.

Who did he think I needed to check with? My husband? Father? Doctor? Apparently, it needed to be okay with someone other than me. He said that I needed to check and make sure it would be okay for me to be traveling with him specifically. I did not understand why he told me this. It felt creepy, and like I was a child who needed to ask permission for a school trip. I was a professional who had traveled extensively for work before, and he treated me like a child. And I heard women talk about similar situations, and being asked even if it was okay for them to travel on one trip as if they never travelled. This is amazing to me, particularly if travel is part of the job requirement.

I have seen women put in positions that play to their weaknesses and put in stretch positions with no safety net. I was personally in a role at one time in my career when a peer was leading projects in survey research. I have extensive experience and expertise in this area in my previous roles and my Ph.D. work. My peer had no experience or expertise in survey research at all, and she hated it. She asked me for help a lot and confided in me that she also asked her husband for help a lot because he was a statistician, as was I.

I asked my boss about being more involved in the research work, and the answer was, "No." No reason was given. I've seen this repeatedly. Why not play to women's strengths and interests? I dare say that in some company cultures, it's another way to ensure frustration, weakness, and failure. I also see patterns of women being promoted with no safety net. This ensures vulnerability.

When I coach women and they are offered a stretch assignment, I ask them to inquire about what happens if they fail. Usually, a man will get a new, safer role if his stretch assignment does not work out, "because he's a good guy." I've seen this repeatedly. But if a woman fails in a stretch assignment, the conversation behind closed doors turns to, "See what happens when we promote a woman? We gave her a chance, and she failed. She can't hack it. She's out." I encourage men and women to ask what type of support, mentoring, and backup plan they have if a stretch assignment does not work out for them.

GINGER-ROGERS-ING

I had a devastating harassment experience one time in my twenties, and I consulted my father about it. My father is retired now, but he had a very successful career while he was working as an engineer, and later as a manager and leader in different industries. I respect his experience, and sometimes I would share my experiences with him and ask for his advice. One time he suggested that I sue the company.

I responded, "But if I do that, I may never work again."

My dad said, "You may not have to."

I wanted to work, and wanted to make a difference. I refused to get bullied out of the workforce. I liked my work, and wanted to keep doing it, but I resented the hassles. That is how most women feel. They enjoy their work, and they want to make a contribution. They just don't feel like they should have to make that contribution while regularly defending themselves. This "constantly defending" themselves adds an extra level of demand on women that is wearisome, as it's meant to be.

Women incessantly strive to balance being strong but not too strong, smart but not too smart, attractive but not too attractive, fun but not too fun, and so on... lest we be severely judged. Women work hard to achieve unachievable and ever-changing societal expectations (Wolf 2002; Petersen 2017). The constant striving and adjusting can feel like carrying around a fifty-pound bag of sand while you are doing your job, shifting it from side to side, trying to keep it camouflaged. Oh, and don't forget to smile. We read cues on how we are supposed to be, then we adjust to try to fit in and succeed.

All of this reading and adjusting is extra effort and extra work. It takes extra mental attention and focus, and it's exhausting. I call this whole process "Ginger-Rogers-ing." Ginger Rogers and Fred Astaire were a dance team in the 1930s. An often-repeated quotation of the cartoonist Bob Thaves says about Fred Astaire, "Sure he was great, but don't forget that Ginger Rogers did everything he [Fred Astaire] did... backwards and in high heels." (Thaves 1983) I'll add that she also never tripped over her long flowing skirts, and she made everything look easy. That's what we do when we smoothly stride through our challenges with grace and apparent ease, invoking the "good girl" image we learned when we were young.

I have seen women held back in their careers for being overly aggressive or too weak, and have had to ask myself, "Would a man with the same behaviors suffered the same fate?" I have wondered if these repetitive patterns are my imagination. Honestly, I have at times hoped it was my imagination, but it's not. Women talk about these things only when we feel safe. We fear retaliation for calling out unfairness, so we act like everything is okay when we are around most of our male colleagues and even many of our female colleagues.

I'm writing this at a time when Donald Trump has been president for thirteen months, and it feels like our broader U.S. culture is sliding backwards in some ways. In some pockets of society, it seems more acceptable to degrade or minimize women today. I've coached and interviewed quite a few mid-career professional women, in particular, mid-career women in their forties to sixties are a resource that many companies do not sufficiently leverage. Mid-career women have much to give and to gain in work environments that are set up for their success. They have life and professional experience and insights, depth and courage, and most have learned to speak up when others can't. Mid-career women are still in very small numbers in leadership positions. We are reaching a tipping point, however, that is critical for making a positive change.

THE BOYS' CLUB

So there we were, Kathy and I, two women working in a manufacturing company in a rural Texas community. I was given a lot of responsibility and free reign in my work and my impression was that the same was true for Kathy. Over the next few months, the company hired two or three more professional women, so there were more women professionals to talk and interact with. It was, overall, a very macho culture. Professional respect was hit or miss, we could not count on being included in important conversations. Sometimes we were included in important meetings, and sometimes we were not. Sometimes we were asked for our opinions, and sometimes we were not. There was definitely a big "boys' club." And I guess we could say there was a "girls' club" but it was very small. They had all the people with power in their club, and all the "up and comers" too. They had swagger and connections. They were the "it group," the "in crowd."

I never saw any woman break into the "boys' club," and I never saw any woman invited in. Women and men play by different sets of rules. Women are polite, collaborative, and sensitive, we pay attention to feelings. Women grow up playing "house" and "tea time," while boys play sports and "war" (Heim, Hughes, and Golant 2015). Traditionally, boys have played sports, and girls started playing sports more after Title IX passed in 1972. Sports participation teaches fairness, competition, teamwork, and rule following - when it's done right.

But girls still play nicer than boys, in general. Parents and other authority figures socialize women to be "sweet," and to not engage in conflict, even constructive conflict. Conflict is too "pushy" and "aggressive." What does the nursery rhyme say? "Girls are sugar and spice and everything nice," and "Boys are snips and snails and puppy dog tails." We learn stereotypes young. Gender roles give license to boys for rough and tough behavior, but the same is not true for girls, who learn that their range of acceptable behaviors is narrow. Boys and girls carry what they've learned into adulthood, where the men and women they become suffer consequences for crossing into the other's gender-based behavioral territory.

When I was young, my mother chastised me repeatedly for being "bold." I had (and still have) a tendency to ask direct questions and look people straight in the eye. My mother never liked it. Once when I was six or seven, I looked straight up into her hazel eyes as she yelled at me for something I'd done.

Almost done with her chewing out, she yelled, "Stop staring at me!"

I lowered my gaze.

"Jesus! You are so bold!" she seethed.

She was socializing me to not be too assertive or pushy. When I was eight or nine years old, my stepfather said he was going to teach me about "tact." He said that it was important to have tact, and told me that, for example, if I wanted to know a woman's age, I should get her talking about high school.

"See if you can get an idea of when she graduated," he said, "or see if she'll say what year she graduated." He told me that it's rude to ask a woman her age, but if you know when a woman graduated from high school, you can calculate it.

"Since most people graduate from high school at seventeen or eighteen years old," he said, "you'll be able to calculate her age."

Bingo! I realized that "tact" was figuring things out without people realizing you were figuring things out. It seemed like being sneaky. My mother interrupted and said, "I don't want her to know things like that! Don't teach her that!"

I reasoned from Mom's reaction that she did not approve of me figuring things out without people realizing it (or being sneaky). I knew at a young age that it wasn't "ok" for me to be "bold" and ask questions directly. Mom communicated that loud and clear. I could not be "tactful" either. I felt confused. How was I supposed to find things out?

Eventually, I realized that my mother did not think it was proper for a woman or girl to know much. Although she was bright and liked being informed, she told me later that being smart made a girl masculine, and that being smart and having an education made a girl a lesbian. Being a lesbian, in her mind, was a fate worse than death. She did not want a daughter of hers to be unfeminine in the most socially unacceptable meaning of the word (in her opinion), and she did not want any daughter of hers to not be traditional marriage material. She planned for each of her daughters to marry a "catch," that would be one of her greatest achievements.

For us to be bold, unfeminine, assertive, bitchy, overweight, unattractive, tomboyish, or slutty was just not acceptable. She told me a hundred times, "You ever come home pregnant I'll put you out on the street with the rest of the garbage! You'll be out! Out on your own."

Sometimes she would say, "You ever do anything to disgrace me, I'll get a gun, and I'll shoot ya. Don't think I won't."

Mom defined what it was to be an acceptable young girl by a narrow path, at least for me she did. I believe that she sensed from the time that I was very young that I was bright and courageous. She didn't like it, and committed to crushing my spirit, in part for my sake and in part for hers. I share these stories because I know I'm not alone. We all have formative experiences growing up. Our parents and siblings socialize us long before we form our reason and logic abilities.

How we are raised impacts our beliefs, and our beliefs run our adult lives. In my career, I've talked with, known, and coached hundreds of professional women and men who are trying to figure out how their gender and gender identity affects their career choices and success and what to do about it. People struggle with issues of what it means to be "good," "a bully," "a dictator," or "nice." We formed these concepts while we were children.

We hold conscious and unconscious beliefs about women, men, feminine energy, masculine energy, and gender roles that impact the workforce and our roles in it. Layers of unconscious interaction occur in every work meeting and interaction. If we look closely at these beliefs, we'll find the root causes of challenges in the workforce today. I've talked with clients, including leaders, who are interested in challenging old beliefs and innovating workplace cultures for more balance and inclusion. Others unconsciously move through their days taking action on unconscious beliefs developed in a family home or on the playground thirty, forty or fifty years ago. Now really, how helpful is that?

In Chapter 2, we looked at the persistent absence of women in top leadership positions. There are several reasons for women's absence, and it's a complex issue. As long as men and women consciously or unconsciously support traditional gender roles and stereotypes, we are not going to make significant progress towards seeing more women leaders in U.S. companies. As long as we do not believe that women can and should successfully lead organizations, we will continue to have small numbers of women in top leadership positions. Men and women still question the ability of women to lead. Yes, we women even question ourselves.

Many girls are born every day with tremendous leadership qualities and the ability to learn to be leaders. And many boys are born with nurturing and intuitive qualities and the ability to learn related behaviors. But, when a parent has a child that is different or special, that parent will often work hard to try to have their child blend in as much as possible to avoid challenges and problems as the child grows up. My mother did this to me. Many parents are not equipped for the challenges of having a special, unique or advanced child (Jaffe and Davidson 2009). The parent encourages what they think is normal or mainstream behavior and works to diminish behaviors that they think are unusual. That is understandable. Gender socialization for children is well documented in research (Bridges 2018; Bem 1983; Honig 1983; Bradley and Gobbart 1989).

When parents raise children according to how they were socialized themselves, social standards can be limiting, or even a generation or two old. When parents raise children in a limiting way, that child may not become ready for the future. They are not ready for changes in the culture, and they are not ready to lead change. As a result, we perpetuate the status quo unconsciously and wonder why we do not see more progress.

American women continue to be raised to be "good girls," to be polite, to defer, to wait to speak until asked or until their turn, and to be non-threatening peace-makers and peace-keepers (Frankel 2014; Heim, Hughes, and Golant 2015). I was. That was my mother's point about not being "bold." When women grow up, we hold onto what we've been taught. Many of us continue our "good girl" behaviors and personas as default personality traits because that is what has been rewarded in school and by friends and parents. It is also what we see in the media. Typically, a woman will not push herself into any "club." It would be incredibly rude. And in most social circles, a woman who is pushy gets the dreaded labels of "bitch," "too aggressive," "ball breaker," "Femi-Nazi," and worse. So most women stay the "nice girl," and reap the repercussions of that as the lesser of two evils. At work, she watches her male colleagues get the better assignments and promotions.

At one of the manufacturing companies I worked at, most days around 11:30 AM a group of six or eight young professional men gathered at the entrance to the parking lot. They formed the "in-group." I'll talk about "in-groups" in the next section. Briefly, an "in-group" is a dominant group with rights and privileges above other groups. From the entrance to the parking lot, they went to lunch. Some of the group changed every day, and some were consistent. There were never any women.

I brought that up in a training session one day. We had about forty-five men participants in class, and about five women. I mentioned the gender-specific lunch group. It was a training class on diversity, so it was fitting. One of the young men in the class said, "Anyone can join us. If someone wants to come, they should join the group."

After at least two decades of training to be "good girls," it was highly unlikely that any professional woman was going to invite herself to lunch with that group and risk being shamed, embarrassed or accused of being inappropriately "ballsy" or "pushy." I suggested that to make it more comfortable it would help to invite a few women directly. My comment was dismissed. Men and women operate differently in social circles. Inclusion continues to be a challenge for companies because of the differences in these social norms.

Experts encourage women to succeed professionally by behaving like men with advice such as, "Just insert yourself into the group. Be one of the guys," or, "Invite yourself. What do you have to lose?" (Heim, Hughes, and Golant 2015; Frankel 2014).

At times, this is great advice. I have given this advice to clients myself. I have also used this advice myself. I call this category of advice for women the, "Act Like A Man" category of advice. It includes jewels such as:

- Lower your voice a tone or two.
- Take up more physical space by spreading your arms out.
- Choose words so that your language is more direct.
- Wear drab colors such as beige, brown and grey.
- Wear clothes that don't show your figure or look too feminine.
- Support decisions with data, data, and more data; use data on profit and loss and productivity (not people - that is too touchy-feely).

The problem is that when we do this, we lose a part of ourselves. We are women. We bring value, as women, to the workplace. Women naturally carry divine feminine energy more strongly than men, just as men naturally carry divine masculine energy more strongly than women. We all have both. When we deny ourselves our birthright of divine feminine energy, we embrace imbalance. We have all paid a price at the hands of women taking this advice. I'll explain more about this in Chapter 6. Men and women deny the feminine within themselves to fit in. This is damaging to all of us.

THE OTHER

The manufacturing company hired Kathy (my supervisor) and me within the same month. We worked in different buildings, and we dressed differently. We had different senses of style. Kathy frequently wore dresses, while I wore casual pants most of the time, and professional separates when I needed to be dressier. My job required that I be in more casual attire.

Kathy was smart, funny and insightful. We did not look alike, but people mistook us for each other constantly. We got called each other's names. We chalked it up to "All white women look alike, right?" Um, no. We don't. It is telling now that people did not pay enough attention to us, to our uniqueness, to be able to tell us apart. I take it as a sign that we were disregarded as unimportant and irrelevant. I'm not sure people even looked at our faces or listened to our voices. If they had, they would have seen how different we were.

I love the piece Gena-Mour Barrett did for BuzzFeed in 2016 titled *How To Tell The Difference Between Me And The Only Other Black Girl Here* on a similar issue. As Barrett writes, all Black girls do not look alike. Extrapolating from Barrett's theme, all Asian people, all Indian people, and all white women in their twenties do not look alike. You can easily tell people apart and remember their names if you pay attention and make an effort — unless they are congenital twins or doppelgängers. Barrett proposes tips like "Pay attention to our voices," and "Notice our completely different personalities." I say focus and make an effort. Kathy and I were not so lucky. That was over twenty years ago. According to Barrett and her personal experience, we can still use help on this today.

Being unable to distinguish between two people from the same under-represented group comes across as rude and insensitive. This behavior demonstrates the belief that, "*They* are all the same," where "they" is "the Other," and means "different from me." Simone de Beauvoir describes this concept as "otherness" in *The Second Sex* (Beauvoir, Borde, and Malovany-Chevallier 2009), which was originally published in 1949. In the western world, people in the mainstream unconsciously (or sometimes consciously) perceive people in the minority or protected groups as "the Other." De Beauvoir wrote of women being the "quintessential Other," always defined in relation to men.

If a white male, for example, is thinking this way at work, he would put all professional women into one bucket conceptually. There would not be a need to distinguish between them or pay attention to details associated with them. Members of "the Other" group blend together. The same white male might put all African Americans into a bucket. He might also have a bucket for lesbians and gay men. This thinking is lazy, as it depends on stereotypes for understanding. Individuals in "Other" buckets get measured against people in the mainstream group, the "in-group." In the most extreme cases, members of "the Other" don't have names or unique details. They are just, "Other." They blend together.

Research on "in-groups" and "out-groups" has been well documented by social scientists for over fifty years (Tajfel 1970; Leyens et al. 2018). An "in-group" is a dominant group with formal and/or informal rights and privileges above other groups. "In-group" members enjoy prestige and status above "out-group" members of the same culture. "In-group" members consider non-members as "the Other." They think of non-members as members of the "out-group." This mental "bucketing" demonstrates a belief that individuals are unexceptional and lacking in dimension. Where Kathy and I worked the young men who went to lunch belonged to the "in-group." The boys' club was the "in-group." The girls' club was the "out-group," or "the Other."

I'm sure Kathy and I were thought of as "those women," or something similar. We belonged to the "out-group." To imply that Kathy and I were indistinguishable, which someone did almost daily, showed a lack of interest or motivation for gaining an understanding of what was unique about each of us, including that we were different people, we looked different, had different jobs, worked in different buildings, and were from different parts of the country. Kathy and I laughed about it, but it was rude and dismissive.

The boys had their club, their "in-group." They did not invite us in, and we did not invite ourselves or push our way in. Day-by-day, two cultures developed. The women's culture stayed small. Women ate lunch together and became friends. The men did the same. Thirty years later, I mostly see the same behavior patterns inside organizations. Unwritten rules and unconscious beliefs continue to guide our behaviors. Sometimes a man steps out of the boys' club, reaches across to the girls' club and champions a woman. We need more of those times.

Alternatively, sometimes men or senior women push women down a few steps, keeping us from achieving our career goals. These slights can be major or minor, but they continue to be pervasive and damaging. They show up as insults, harassment, bullying, condescension, jokes at a woman's expense, sophomoric behavior, and belittling. These behaviors serve to keep women "in their place," in the "out-group." Just in the last year or two, I've seen more women having less tolerance for these behaviors. Women speak up more and stand up for ourselves. We are sensitive to subtle and overt attempts to demean us. All harassment is not egregious. I'll give you some examples.

IT'S A MAN'S WORLD

I have heard stories of harassment, bullying, belittling and more from hundreds of women for over twenty years. The stories come from women who work all over the world and in different industries and disciplines - engineering, IT, human resources, law, and more.

Women who have more job security and more options are more likely to stand up for themselves and tell bullies and harassers to stop their insulting behaviors, or these women will leave bad situations. When these women speak out, they help the women who cannot. Many women need their jobs and the benefits that their jobs provide them and their families. For many women, speaking up would open them up to risks that they cannot afford to take, and so what they must do is stay quiet.

Twenty years ago, I never anticipated that such violations and gaffes would still be prevalent in a 2017 workplace. When anyone in the workplace is diminished and limited, it hurts us all. It hurts businesses, and it hurts professionals working in those businesses. It limits business growth, limits job growth and hurts productivity. It affects our economy and our culture. It needs to stop. I recommend we constructively spend our time valuing what women bring to the workplace instead of chipping away at them and undermining their confidence and sense of security.

And we cannot just blame men. Women do not always support each other. We have barely begun to integrate everything that is valuable about having women in the workforce as professionals and leaders. We have much to capitalize on here.

Of the hundreds of women I have professionally coached in my career, I remember very few, extremely few, being regretful, bitter, or resentful. They want a chance to work, contribute and use their brains. They want to provide for their families. They have a resounding desire to "not get anyone into trouble." I wish I had a dollar for every time I've heard a woman tell me, "I just don't want to get anyone in trouble." Women want to be challenged, valued and respected. They are willing to invest time and effort into helping workplaces be productive. We ignore insults and indiscretions, forgive and forget. Eventually, there comes a time when we can't take it anymore, and we are burned out. I've been there myself, so I understand.

I had a coaching session with one of my clients yesterday. She's a brilliant Ph.D. chemist in a global manufacturing company in Houston. She told me that her mentor, a woman in her fifties, prefaces advice by saying that in the workplace, "It's a man's world," and so we women have to adjust and modify our perspectives and behaviors to accommodate that world.

My mother used to tell me that. I can hear her saying it, "It's a man's world, so get used to it."

Hear this: I reject that position.

It's Everyone's World. Women have contributed in the sciences, technologies, in engineering, and math, in the arts, and in business for hundreds of years. Let's stop with this ludicrous idea that the world of science, business, art, medicine, and higher education is "a man's world." Women are graduating from college and business programs in higher numbers than men. We are hired by companies in higher or equal numbers to men. In mid-career, the numbers change - there are more men. I've talked with company leaders who are interested in learning how to keep women in their companies. They want to be able to hire, retain, and engage women in equal numbers to men all the way to the boardroom and retirement. Some leaders realize the benefits to creativity and innovation that diversity brings to their organizations. They want to know how to solve the problem of too many mid-career women exiting the workforce.

So, what is the answer? We'll get to that in Chapters 9, 11, 12 and 13. First, let's examine what is happening at the macro level in our culture. This is where we are seeing many drivers for change. And these drivers affect company cultures.

"

IT'S EVERYONE'S WORLD.
INCLUSION SUPPORTS
CREATIVITY, INNOVATION, AND TEAMWORK.
—Lisa Liszcz

4

Politics – The Big Stage

CHAPTER 4

FIRST WOMAN RUNS FOR PRESIDENT OF THE UNITED STATES

My heart exploded with joy and excitement when Hillary Rodham Clinton ran for president in 2016 and received the nomination for the Democratic Party. I experienced the excitement and wonder of a kid visiting the beach for the first time, and an unexpected sense of freedom, pride, and importance in my womanness. I sensed I mattered more than I had ever mattered. I have understood my whole life about the importance of role models, but I never experienced anything like I did when she got nominated. When I thought about it I grew giddy, breathless and almost weightless. Her nomination shocked me. Part of me had believed I would never see this in our country.

For decades, Hillary repulsed me. Bill did too. I grew into appreciating Hillary, and it surprised me. Then I became rabid, like a former smoker. Once I came to appreciate Hillary, I did support her, enthusiastically. I donated to her campaign, and I supported her on social media. Every time she had a presidential debate with Donald Trump, I looked forward to it, and I reveled in viewing it. She represented me and every girl I'd ever known who super-prepared for every task and job. To me, she depicted a warrior who had fought in battles for decades for the rights of women, children, veterans, public servants, and for herself and her family. I did not agree with everything she had done, not by a long shot. But I did admire her. I still do. She was the right person at the right time, and I gave her my support.

It was exhilarating to see a woman run for President of the United States. I absorbed every detail. Women who work in male dominated environments, or in traditionally male roles, know how scrutinized and judged we are by men and by other women. I observed how she and her staff carefully managed her message as well as her demeanor, voice, tone, makeup, hair, jewelry, and attire day after day after day. I realized how smart and thoughtful she was. It fascinated me to follow her campaign unfold and observe what so many of us believed we were seeing - the election of the first woman President of the United States of America. My excitement was palpable. It had taste. It vibrated in every pore of my body, and the summer of 2016 was exhilarating for me. I knew Hillary was not the best candidate in the world, but she was the best of our options. She was experienced, smart, and prepared. The polls consistently reported that she would win the election.

And yet I had doubts. Donald Trump surprised me at every news cycle. His winning his party nomination over other exceedingly qualified nominees astounded me. His competitiveness, the polls shocked me. He made gaffes like when he mocked a disabled reporter, or said he could shoot someone in Times Square and still get elected. And he continued to rise in the polls. I never saw anything like the 2016 election before, and it worried me.

Friends and acquaintances of mine — intelligent, sophisticated women — said they could not stand Hillary's voice. Hillary sounded shrill, they said. They were uncomfortable with the idea of a woman president. They said that Hillary came with too much "baggage," referring to Bill Clinton's time in office and some of Hillary's history. Deep down in me, an ache started to grow, a sense of panic that Hillary might not win. It left me with a fear that Trump would continue to beat all odds and surprise everyone on election day.

When women talked about Hillary's "baggage," it infuriated me. Voters evaluated Hillary in large part based on her husband and her marriage. Women and men were going to limit her based on what her husband had done and how she had reacted. Because of that, we would exclude her from the opportunity to work independently on the biggest stage available to her, even though she was ready for it and was our best choice.

In contrast, Donald Trump's history of failed businesses, bankruptcies, lawsuits against him, divorces, and sexual harassment and assault accusers slid right off him like water off a duck's back. Yes, the undercurrent demanding a change in our country was strong, and Hillary was part of a political dynasty. But it is very hard for me to imagine that misogyny did not play a role in our failure to elect her as our first woman president. Our country fundamentally is willing to overlook many failures and discretions of a man. But we reject women who are too strong, too bright, too daring, and too uppity. And that is what happened.

I never thought I'd see in my lifetime a woman nominated to run for a major political party for President of the United States. We all need role models. Role models give our brains the capacity to envision that we can do something bigger than we have imagined before. On June 7, 2016, the night that Hilary made her acceptance speech for clinching the nomination, I stayed up way past my bedtime to watch her make that speech on TV. She walked out wearing suffragette white while her staff blared Katy Perry's Roar over the sound system.

I cried like a baby. Because of my own experiences and how I was raised (I'll write about this in Chapter 8), I am keenly aware of the misogyny in this country. I thought I was watching a miracle. I felt the fight of thousands of women for over 160 years in this country mattered. Their fight was not in vain, it was clear we had moved the needle after all. Women could be seen as intellectual, strong and wise leaders. I grew to be hopeful that while we would not have a perfect president, we would have a compassionate president who would bring judgment and experience to the White House and would bring a vision for moving our country forward with strength as well as empathy and heart. She was the right one. Hillary is fierce. She is formidable and tough. At that moment, I burst with pride for her, and I burst with pride for our country.

I realized in my heart and soul that any little girl in this country really could be anything she dreamed of. My body filled with hope and joy. I realized that with Hillary as president, every little girl in this country would have her as a role model. Hillary would inspire young girls and women, giving foundation to their dreams and aspirations.

I understood in my bones and every fiber of my being how so many people in the African-American communities of our country were affected by having the Obamas as the first family of the United States, and how meaningful that was. While I appreciated President Obama and his family very much, I could see now for the first time how Obama's presidency could mean more to African-Americans living in the United States. I experienced that now with Hillary. It touched me to see a smart, tenacious woman celebrated and promoted in a way I had never seen before. And I felt celebrated and promoted too. I felt empowered and energized by what she and her campaign accomplished that night. This was so big and so exciting. It was history. It was everything.

I found new strength in my voice. What I had to say sounded more credible to my ears, I heard more validity and power in what I said. It was not a huge shift. The shift in my gut, although small, burned like a fire. It had fierceness in it. I remembered being young and bold. I remembered my mother saying to me, "You are so bold," and her saying it as a criticism. But this boldness brought me strength. As a little girl, I'd tamped my boldness down, and now it bubbled up and wanted voice. I wanted to give it voice, and I wasn't a little girl anymore.

PRESIDENT TRUMP

In 2016, Donald Trump and Hillary Clinton ran a competitive and ugly race for President of the United States. Americans came to be demoralized by the condition to which politics deteriorated. The rhetoric grew into a steady stream of abysmal chatter. Neither candidate represented, in many people's opinions, an optimal leader. Hillary had a long history in politics, and the public was sick of her and her former president husband. Hillary and Bill were scandal ridden, and Americans wanted a fresh start. Donald, a bombastic, egotistical, unpredictable reality TV show host and commercial real estate developer had a record of misogynistic behaviors for which he offered no apology. During the campaign, polls reported that Hillary would win. Everywhere we looked, we received news about Hillary being ahead...until election night.

Donald won according to the Electoral College vote, which many call an outdated system. Hillary won the popular vote. Donald was elected President of the United States on November 7, 2016, after a nasty campaign in which he demonstrated no understanding of, or clear plans for, domestic or foreign policy. He won on a ball cap slogan - Make America Great Again. How did this happen?

The result of the 2016 presidential election is complex. The outcome was brewing for decades. Political, social, economic, and other factors set the stage for Trump's win. I'll let others analyze other dimensions of the election's complexity. Relative to how people in our country perceive men and women, the outcome makes sense. I'll explore male and female energies in depth in Chapter 6. For now, I briefly summarize that in our country we are not big champions of feminine energy. People who highly value male energy as the solution for our country elected Trump. They made sure that a woman did not join the ultimate "boys' club" or "in-group."

During the election, here are what some men and women in the media, and who I met with in person, said about Hillary:

- "I can't see having a woman for president."
- "I don't know if a woman is capable of protecting our country."
- "I can't stand her voice. It's too shrill."
- "I don't like how she does her hair."
- "She's a grandma. A grandma can't be president."
- "I don't like it when she starts to yell. It makes me nervous."
- "She looks little on the stage next to Donald."

These statements show disdain for what is feminine. A woman's voice is naturally higher. It's softer. It does not mean it comes from a person who is not strong and will not protect. On the contrary, when a woman goes into mama bear mode to protect a child or another loved one, she is vicious and strong. In part, people gravitated towards Donald Trump as a leader because of his height. It is well-documented that people gravitate towards taller people when selecting leaders, especially for president (Lindqvist 2012; Stulp et al. 2013). In a male-identified society with male-identified politics, height will be perceived more positively than petiteness. It stands to reason that some people unconsciously perceived Donald Trump to be the better leader.

We are under such a spell of male superiority in this country that we cannot even recognize female leadership qualities. Female strength, coupled with intelligence and power, is a divine source for protection, safety, and guidance. We let our contempt for softness and vulnerability get in the way of understanding what real leadership is. Instead, we focus on hair, voice, height, and other features that don't matter. We are intolerant of aging skin and gray hair on women. Women are expected to spend inordinate amounts of time and money to appear unnaturally youthful and attractive. And Hillary did it all. She looked great, prepared, ran a great campaign, and lost to an unprepared, inexperienced, bloated, fat, wrinkled old man with bad skin, bad hair, and misogynistic attitudes.

It was not her specifically. It was Her. It was that she was Female. It was the feminine that people couldn't elect as President of the United States of America. Her being a woman was not the entire reason Hillary lost. Elections present many complexities, this factor was one of many. We had voters who consciously or unconsciously voted against her because she was a woman. They voted against the feminine. Voters wanted a president with a penis, whether it came with a brain or not. Vagina with brain = no. Penis sans brain = yes. Voters declared, "It is a man's world."

We live in a culture where women are limited for no other reason than being women. Our culture limits women in pervasive and egregious ways. This is not hyperbole. It's not a whiny or illegitimate claim. It is objectively true. It happens more than we care to admit. To make a change, we must first understand our current situation.

It broke my heart into a million pieces that the Electoral College of the United States elected Donald Trump president in 2016. It was a misguided choice based on faulty reasons. Led by the desire for an unspecified change and unconscious preferences for male leadership, people placed their votes for a misogynistic bully who was ill-prepared for leading the free world.

The results of the election stunned me. I knew in my gut that part of the reason that Trump was elected was because he was a man. I understood that our country, to its detriment, cannot embrace the feminine divine and, in fact, repels it. This realization made me miserable. It became clear to me how out of balance we are as a country and how malignant our current state is. The full impact of this realization had not registered with me until the election results. It filled me with terror. Then a desire to speak out gripped me. That desire blossomed into a bigger desire and a passion for being part of change, and for illuminating challenges we are facing and solutions to those challenges.

LEADERS SHOULD BE MEN

We only prefer male leaders in politics, right?

In business, higher education, the arts, law, etc., we embrace the diversity of feminine energy in leadership, right?

Wrong.

I've heard hundreds of accounts from men and women about preferring male leaders. I've dealt with this issue myself personally. Many women "male-identify" in order to be more successful in business. (I'll write more about this in Chapter 10.) When we do this, we undermine everyone's success. I want to share with you one encounter where a woman shared with me her feelings on male and female leaders. This example represents a common perspective.

I went to a coffee shop recently, and I took my computer with me to work on this book. I saw my friend, Olivia, and she approached me and asked what I was writing. I'm not good with ages, but I know that Olivia is older than I am. She is thin and graceful. She used to work as a ballet dancer in New York City and the long lines of her body reflect that.

She asked me, "What is your book about?"

I find that question difficult to answer quickly.

"Feminism," I said.

I understand now that I had always projected onto Olivia some level of political liberalism. I guess I assumed she was liberal because she lived in New York City and worked in the arts.

She asked me, "Oh, are you one of those?"

"Yes, I am," I smiled, "are you?"

"I believe that leaders should be men," she answered.

I gasped. The breath was knocked out of me as I looked at her wide-eyed.

She replied, "It's been that way since the beginning of time. It's tradition. You must've been disappointed when Hillary lost the election."

"I was devastated. I could not believe that our country elected someone with zero government experience," was my reply.

She said that she had been surprised too, and that she had conflicted feelings about the election.

"But," she repeated, "a leader needs to be a man. It's always been that way." I said I disagreed, and she changed the subject to more common ground.

She told me she was upset about what was happening at the New York City Ballet. She had been keeping up with the story about Peter Martins, the Ballet's master-in-chief who was under investigation for physical and verbal abuse allegations (Pogrebin 2018). Martins retired suddenly in January 2018 after more than thirty years of leading the ballet. For decades, women who worked for Martins had accused him of misconduct. Martins had also been accused of spousal abuse. He was under investigation at the time of his retirement.

Olivia shared with me that she was furious that his behavior had been tolerated. She said, "That is my ballet. I am totally disgusted and furious that his behavior has been allowed for so long. It is inexcusable." She thought the board should have done something much sooner.

While Olivia appreciates male leadership and sees that as an important tradition, she recognizes the challenges some men have in leadership roles. While she talked, I sensed her frustration and inner conflict. She wants men to lead, and she wants them to be good leaders. Many women I've talked to have this in common. She said the next master-in-chief would probably be a woman, and she was uncomfortable with that possibility. So many of us are not used to seeing women leaders yet and don't look forward to seeing them.

During the 2016 presidential campaign, I talked to women who were frustrated and conflicted. Some of my friends, clients, and colleagues expressed a similar frustration to what Olivia shared. Since we still do not see and experience a significant number of women in leadership roles, women still have strong, visceral reactions to women in leadership when they do show up.

I am referring to women from all walks of life. I have talked with women with high school educations who are living in rural areas, and women in urban areas who have graduate degrees. I have talked with women who are professionals with successful careers and with women who have happily served as wives and mothers. I have heard from a diverse selection of women that a woman's voice, stature, mannerisms, attire, hairdo and/or presence or lack of sexuality or sensuality is a deal breaker for them for leadership. We saw tectonic shifts begin in our culture in 2017. These macro shifts lay the groundwork for change in company cultures.

66

IT'S TIME TO BREAK THE SPELL OF BELIEF IN
MALE SUPERIORITY.
WE ALL BRING VALUABLE
TALENTS AND SKILLS TO LIFE.
—Lisa Liszcz

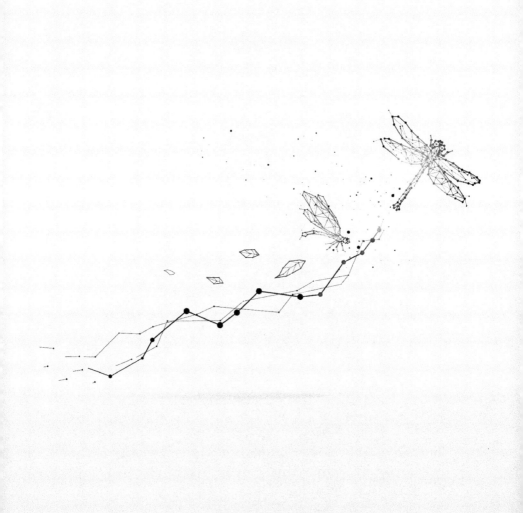

5

Women's Voices – Loud & Proud

CHAPTER 5

SEXUAL ASSAULT IN THE NEWS

In 2017, a women's movement of feminine emergence started. This movement's roots grew out of previous women's movements, and got ignited by various court cases and Hillary Clinton's loss for President of the United States. A few seminal cases and the presidential election led to a tipping point which I'll discuss more in Chapter 7. Feminine emergence is the surfacing and positioning of feminine energy and ideals across the globe. A collective bubbling up of feminine energy and consciousness feeds this movement.

The first seeds of this movement were planted with the Anita Hill testimony in 1991. The next major milestone came in November 2014, when NBC dropped Bill Cosby, an American stand-up comedian, actor, musician and author, from a major project, and the TV Land television network pulled reruns of the Bill Cosby show. Both networks acted in response to allegations against Cosby of decades of using narcotics to drug women and then assault them (Kyle, Littlefield and Etehad 2017). This case got my attention because it was an early case where allegations of assault in the entertainment industry were taken with seriousness, and the perpetrator was facing serious business and life consequences.

We have historically seen allegations made and then cases settled with no substantive career consequences for the perpetrator, who then does his best to gaslight the situation and make the accuser(s) appear to be hysterical, overly emotional or over-reactive. Sometimes, the media or perpetrator questions the accuser's mental state or sense of reality.

In 1991, Anita Hill testified at the Clarence Thomas Senate Judiciary Committee hearing for Supreme Court Justice. Fourteen men questioned her for three days. She shared details of sexual harassment that was offensive to her committed by Clarence Thomas while she worked for him. Senators assassinated her character, accused her of lying, and said she was acting out of disappointment from being rejected by men in her life (Suro 1991; Roberts 2016). One pundit described Anita as, "a little bit nutty and a little slutty" (Gray 2016). Thomas denied the allegations, and Anita stuck by her word. By the end of the three days, Americans believed Clarence Thomas over Anita Hill two-to-one.

I remember those hearings. I believed Anita Hill. She appeared to be a smart, conscientious woman reluctantly telling the truth. Under oath, she answered questions she took seriously. A lawyer and a law professor, Anita held up to exhaustive questioning and never got emotional. Anita explained in a steadfast, poised style that people needed to know the truth.

I was working at a chemical plant in a rural community outside of Houston, Texas, and my colleagues and I agreed that what Anita described resembled what happened in our work environment. Men protested, sometimes actively, when turned down for a date. Colleagues made sexual jokes and innuendos. Comments similar to what Anita described about pubic hair and Coke cans, and jokes or references about penis size and virility occurred. The Senators who accused Anita of telling boldfaced lies and falsifying activities in the Department of Education were out of touch or gas-lighting. The Senate confirmed Clarence Thomas, but when the hearings were over, a small change had occurred. One woman had spoken up.

We got a glimpse of what bravery looks like. She appeared dignified, smart and bold. Yet, our culture continued with almost no changes; jokes and what Melania Trump called "boy talk" continued. But all workplaces implemented "preventing sexual harassment" training and the hearings defined a "hostile work environment." For the next twenty-plus years, professional women and the men they worked with played a rotten game where the men would continue their behavior with a "wink-wink, nudge-nudge" that meant, "You won't report me and get me in trouble, right? If not, I'll pretend to accept you as 'one of the guys,' and you'll sort of be 'in the club.'"

Harassment, and in some cases assault, continued in all industries. Women expected this, and until we felt we deserved better and took huge risks, we always would. In 2014, enough credible women stepped forward on the Bill Cosby case that his managers could not make the accusations go away. That was the first case of sexual assault in the public eye with real consequences for the defendant, not just a slap on the wrist. The time had come for sexual assault and women's protection and dignity to matter.

This was the first time that a famous and esteemed member of the "boys' club" publicly faced the consequences for attacking a woman, and in this case, women. There was no way out. There was no way to tell twenty-nine women disparate in age, race, and region they had somehow imagined the same experience, made up the same lie, or had the same fantasies that led to their testimonies (Senators accused Anita Hill of having fantasies that fed her testimony). Here, strength came from numbers, and this case got the public's attention.

WAKING UP

We saw a big year for women's rights in 2017, in part, in reaction to the November 2016 election. Women pulled together and mobilized on January 21, the day after President Trump's inauguration, with a national women's march. Women marched in solidarity and vocalized our rights and our power as women. It was a positive movement across the country and around the world. Women, men, children, and couples of all ages and races marched with signs expressing support for traditionally feminine issues. The issues included women's reproductive rights, right to healthcare, immigration rights, same-sex marriage rights, environmental protection and more.

I took part on that beautiful sunshiny day in Houston. It was an amazing experience. The air buzzed with the energy of everyone there. Love and respect enveloped miles of streets as friends and strangers smiled at each other's signs and slowly walked and talked the march trail. My friend and I took pictures and enjoyed seeing small children, elderly people, people in wheelchairs, gay couples, men, and traditional families all taking part. And there were lots and lots of women. That day, we joined in the largest demonstration of any kind in Houston's history. That afternoon, I watched coverage on the news of the massive marches all over the world. Solidarity of women and men over issues so important to me filled my heart with joy. That day soothed the wound of Tuesday, November 8, 2016, like a salve.

Boldness bubbled up inside the global marchers that day. Like the boldness inside me, their boldness wanted a voice - it came out in sign slogans and loud chants. The marchers could no longer bury their fierceness. Hillary gave us that. She showed us how to be strong and bold. I thought she needed to be president to give us that strength, but she didn't. The fight she fought empowered and inspired millions of people across the globe.

The election woke us up. People put down their phones and got off their couches to make signs, march, and chant. It was beautiful.

Many of us walk through life in a fog, moving from day to day in our routines and assuming other people will take care of important matters such as our rights and safety. The 2016 presidential election results shocked many people out of their fog. People asked, "How could this have happened?" Hilary won the popular vote by almost three million votes and lost the Electoral College vote. People. Woke. Up. They came out of their fog. People awoke to what they often regard as a feminine agenda and embraced it. People marched for diplomacy, love, and peace. It was a feminine emergence.

People said the January 21, 2017 marches aligned with a liberal or democratic agenda. I saw it more as feminine. It amazed me how peaceful all the marches were. In Houston, our march was not only peaceful, it was friendly. People smiled and laughed while taking pictures of each other's signs and T-shirts. Some signs said, "Love it, don't grab it," "Kindness matters," "Nasty women make history," and "Tiny hands can't hold us down." Some of my favorite t-shirts said, "Don't mess with Texas women," and "Nasty women keep fighting."

The messages promoted feminine energy. We waved and hollered our thanks to security and police officers along the route. We petted horses from the local police department's mounted patrol unit. Love and camaraderie showed up that day. There was no hate, anger or fear. There was just a high level of positive energy from inspired people ready to create change by speaking up and being bold. People marched to make a difference on issues they cared about and that mattered to them and their families.

This feminine energy of the marches persisted through 2017 and continues now. I say, "Bravo!" to my brothers and sisters who create change by telling their truth and standing up for what's right. Because women are speaking up about harassment and assault, powerful men in the entertainment, news, arts, and sports industries are losing their jobs and losing business deals.

We are seeing the consequences. Women are ending the era of silence. In October 2017, five women accused Mark Halperin of NBC News of sexual harassment and/or assault. NBC released Halperin, who had been a powerful political pundit in Washington, DC for decades. Four women accused Mario Batali of sexual misconduct in December 2017, and Batali stepped away from his restaurant empire and TV show for a leave of absence.

Fox News released Bill O'Reilly in April 2017 after making an exorbitant settlement of $32 million on behalf of O'Reilly in defense of sexual harassment charges. Sponsors of the show made a mass exodus after the news broke, and the network released the popular host. The network had a fifteen-year history of paying settlements for sexual harassment claims against O'Reilly (Steel and Schmidt 2017).

After many women came forward with sexual harassment and assault charges against Harvey Weinstein, the board of The Weinstein Company (TWC) ousted producer Harvey Weinstein from the company and its board in October 2017.

Large and influential companies like Apple, Lexus, and Amazon followed by breaking all ties with TWC.

Producers canceled major projects for actor Kevin Spacey and comedian Louis C.K., and HBO removed Spacey from the popular House of Cards series after plaintiffs made allegations against both men in 2017.

In a prominent sports case, a court tried Dr. Lawrence Nassar, found him guilty and sentenced him to prison for over 150 years on charges of sexually abusing gymnasts from Michigan State and the U. S. Olympic Team. The judge in this case allowed over 150 accusers to testify in court during the sentencing phase of this trial in January 2018. (Note that at the time of this writing, Nassar is no longer a physician. Michigan revoked his license for three years.)

The momentum at which women spoke out against being controlled by powerful men peaked in January 2018, when The Wall Street Journal released its first reports on the "Stormy Daniels, Donald Trump" scandal. News outlets reported details of the President of the United States allegedly having his personal lawyer and 2016 presidential campaign staff member pay hush money to adult film star, Stormy Daniels (Rothfeld 2018).

The press treated Ms. Daniels and this story with respect. This story had gravitas. We'd come a long way since the hearings in 1991 where congressmen dismissed Anita Hill. CBS News and Anderson Cooper dedicated a full 60 Minutes television show to an interview with Ms. Daniels (Calderone 2018). The interview focused on the alleged affair, but also threats against Ms. Daniels and her child, attempted cover-ups by the Trump campaign, non-disclosure agreements, and bribes.

Ms. Daniels came forward despite threats against her on behalf of the most powerful man in the world. She showed tremendous courage, refusing to let herself be bullied. Stormy stood up for herself and her child, and the world got to watch. I say good for her! Some call Stormy a hero, and I agree (Norman 2018). She's a hero for standing up to a bully. She is a hero for standing up for herself and for telling the truth. This strength is part of feminine emergence.

What is the catalyst for this momentum? Some call this new direction "The Weinstein Effect" (Cooney 2018). The Weinstein case did not start the phenomenon of women reporting sexual abuse at work. Men have sexually harassed and assaulted women at work forever. Some women have reported harassment and assault, but not in these numbers.

Why are so many women coming forward now? Why are women speaking up now? Women who spoke up in 2017 and 2018 said they had hesitated before because they feared retaliation. In my role as an HR professional for over twenty-five years working in large global companies, I heard this from women regularly. Women felt that if they told the truth about harassment or assault they experienced, they would not receive protection. Sometimes they did not feel others would believe them. I felt the same way when I experienced harassment. And we saw this with Anita Hill. Senators questioned Anita's honesty, describing her as someone who either fantasized the stories she told or someone who lied. Even Anita said in her testimony that she worried about retaliation and that was why she hesitated in coming forward sooner. Anita also said the behaviors she endured were typical in her environment and were part of the culture. Anita spoke up and told the truth about Clarence Thomas' character when the issue became bigger than herself.

In 2016, we had the presidential election. It profoundly affected men and women who embraced a consciousness that is not exceedingly masculine. Anyone who saw the capability, desire and tenacity of Hillary during the campaign, and appreciated her centrist approach (sometimes hawkish and at other times compassionate and diplomatic), could also see that pockets of our population maligned her for being a woman. These pockets rejected her as a leader in part because she was a woman. They rejected her voice, mannerisms, height, and shape. They rejected her pantsuits and her stories about being a mother and a grandmother.

Those of us who embody a balance of feminine and masculine energy, and those of us who embrace and value the feminine divine energy, felt our boldness bubbling up. We knew Hilary had won the popular vote. And we knew an unqualified, unintelligent bloviating bully became President. We were done. We'd had it. We were sick and tired of women being dismissed, minimized and disregarded. We could no longer accept our country's aversion for the feminine. We knew we needed balance in our society, culture, businesses, and politics, and we were ready to march, speak up and file complaints if we needed to. The issues expanded to be, as with Anita Hill, much bigger than any individual. Momentum swelled. And we had each other. We were not alone.

In 2017, women in high-visibility professions (like news, sports, and entertainment) stopped worrying about retaliation and filed lawsuits and complaints of sexual harassment and assault in large numbers. The numbers gave women power. Survivors surrounded and supported each other. In the news and entertainment industries, in particular, there were women with enough clout and power to demand action and results. The zeitgeist energized women to step into our power and say, "No more. We are done."

And the feminine emerged. Energies are shifting. Let's learn more about both and about balance.

66

ENERGY IS SHIFTING.
FEMININE EMERGENCE IS IN THE ZEITGEIST.
—Lisa Liszcz

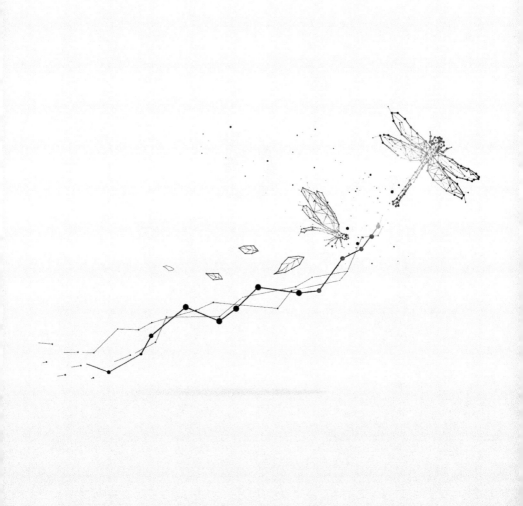

6

The Feminine
and The Masculine

CHAPTER 6

WHAT IS FEMININE ENERGY?

I've introduced the words feminine and divine feminine. I use these terms interchangeably. Feminine energy is surfacing around the world. We see this in the strength and power that women are stepping into in the United States. Hillary Clinton's run for president strengthened the rising tide of divine feminine energy. In her, we found a much-needed role model, an imperfect but strong and smart woman who got exceedingly close to the top executive role in our country.

Elements of the divine feminine include compassion, a worldview, environmental focus, creativity, embracing emotions, intuition, and win-win solutions. We engage in feminine energy when we are kind, nurturing, or vulnerable. We channel our feminine energy when we protect the weak and fight for causes larger than ourselves. When a person or a group embrace these energies, honors and lives them, we move society forward in ways we could not before. We have seen this with leaders such as John F. Kennedy Jr., Martin Luther King Jr., Mother Teresa, and Gandhi.

The U.S. has become over masculinized. We disregard much of what is feminine in our culture, sometimes to the point of loathing what is feminine. We've gotten out of balance, but we are coming back into balance now. There is a movement to embrace, stand up for, and protect the softer energies in both men and women for the benefit of individuals and our society. Our marches and activism in 2016-2018 prove this.

Compassion and empathy add depth to communications, relationships, and negotiations. These abilities in which women tend to be stronger, but men are certainly capable of, help move people forward in business and personal relationships. Our best leaders in all industries show and are known for their compassion and empathy. Emotional intelligence distinguishes the best leaders (Goleman, Boyatzis, and McKee 2013).

Our best leaders embrace a divine feminine worldview and a strong environmental focus. They care deeply about the earth, our parks, water, food supplies and the future of our planet. As human consciousness develops, we grow more egoless and become more motivated to serve. We desire to protect who and what cannot protect themselves or itself, including people who are vulnerable and the planet. When working within divine feminine energy, we want to use our strength and power to protect and serve. Our focus shifts from "me" to "we." Feminine energy wields tremendous strength and power. This power is not destructive. It is constructive. Robert K. Greenleaf, author of *Servant Leadership: A Journey Into The Nature of Legitimate Power and Greatness*, describes servant leadership as leadership where the primary focus is on empowering and building up other individuals and communities. Servant leaders focus on nurturing others, and their organizations improve with increased employee engagement, improved team performance, and increased profits (Schwantes 2016).

Creativity and innovation arise from feminine energy. The world of new ideas, inspiration, and intuition works best when we align with and tap into nonphysical energies. For men and women, embracing and developing the feminine, or "yin," part of themselves yields more opportunities to align with the nonphysical. When we engage with these energies and release to them (i.e., surrender), we allow ourselves to receive inspiration. We correctly perceive passivity to be feminine, but don't confuse passivity with weakness. Surrender requires the courage to be vulnerable and trust the Universe. Surrender invites intuition's voice and invokes creativity and innovation. In my work as a consultant and coach and in my 25 years working in large global companies, creativity and innovation were needed for problem-solving and staying competitive. We can enjoy and benefit from embracing our God-given (or Universe given, or Nature given...however you want to call it) gifts in these areas.

Women and men strong in the feminine energies and related skills are masterful relationship builders, and people love being around them and working with them. Many women are naturally gifted with this emotion-focus and sensitivity, and when they pay attention to it, this skill supports them in their personal and professional lives. They focus on maintaining everyone's self-esteem, particularly when a conflict arises. Win-win solutions allow both parties in a conflict or negotiation to walk away feeling good regarding the result. Both parties walk away feeling respected, with their self-esteem intact, and feeling they got something out of the discussion. They did not get everything. They had to compromise. But they did not lose. They walk away empowered and willing to come back and talk again. As a bonus, they've moved the relationship to the next level.

To engage in feminine energy, one must let go of the ego part of the psyche, at least for a while. I've witnessed men and women leaders who demonstrate this energy. They are mature and wise people who are caring and kind. They care for their employees, colleagues, and organizations. When they care for an individual, they care for the whole individual, not just what that person can contribute at work.

Strength and confidence can come from feminine energy. That is why one can lay down the ego when engaging feminine energy and still have power. Feminine power, the strength that comes from feminine energy, is quiet and strong. Think of a mama wolf stalking prey that will provide food for her cubs. When she hunts, she is strong, quiet, smooth, and graceful. Think of that same mama wolf caring for her cubs — firm, warm, and comforting. Female power is organic, fertile, integrated, wise, quiet, receptive, and soft. This power says, "I will take care of you. I will walk with you, not in front of you, and we will do this together." It says, "I've got your back."

People with divine feminine power share power and allow power to multiply. Shared power includes the power to eat, work, be healthy, or learn and grow.

When I say, "I will walk with you and shepherd you through this process," I share my power, and my power becomes exponential. I know I don't own my power, so I feel no hesitation in sharing it.

When I talk of feminine energy and feminine power, I am not referring to sexuality. "Virgin" and "whore" thinking of women perpetuates insufficient and false concepts of feminine energy. The objectification of women in our culture hurts everyone by rejecting the expansive, beautiful and fruitful aspects of our humanity. The feminine energy that lives in each of us, that we are born with and that we reject in this society, is poised to give us a gold mine of unrealized gifts, talent, and healing. We merely need to open up to it.

WHAT IS MASCULINE ENERGY?

Masculine energy contains action; it is outwardly focused. Ego drives masculine energy. It exudes external power. Masculine energy focuses on the physical world and what is concrete such as data, physical structures, plans and physical money. Masculine energy competes and resolves issues with win-lose paradigms.

When we compete, we use masculine energy or "yang." Masculine energy deconstructs, it aims to destroy what it classifies as "bad" or what it wants but cannot have. When we act to dominate, we act from masculine energy. Masculine energy can be protective and providing. When we focus on external issues and information and away from our gut feelings, conscience or intuition, we use masculine energy. When we feel driven, independent, aggressive, confident, and strong, we are in our masculine energy. We engage our masculine energy when we need to be analytical, systematic, linear, objective, hard, technical or direct.

Masculine energy has served our communities and country well at times. At other times, integration of more feminine energy in decision-making and policy development would have served us much better. I am not poo-pooing or criticizing masculine energy. I am an advocate of masculine energy. It has served me well. I find it invigorating and fun. Our society needs both energies. As a poet, artist, and speaker, Cleo Wade says about masculine and feminine energy, "It all goes back to the old saying: Men and women are like your left and right feet — they're different, but you need them both to get from place to place." (Lester-Coll 2016). We need both in our world. We are most powerful when we consciously choose masculine and feminine energies for the right condition and purpose. This is consciousness.

Historically, masculine energy has dominated the U.S. culture. We function unconsciously in masculine energy most of the time. As a culture, we reject feminine energy in almost every situation from politics to business, education to healthcare, in relationships, in religion, entertainment and in social situations. We do this unconsciously and, therefore, automatically. We do not see feminine energy and feminine power as viable choices on how to behave, think, feel and conduct ourselves. I stumbled into this trap myself.

REJECTING THE FEMININE

Disdain for the feminine shows up when we criticize others by saying:

- "You throw like a girl," or you do anything like a girl.
- "Quit being a baby," (when someone is sensitive).
- "Those are 'girly' colors," (when someone wears pastel, bright, or light-colored clothes).

It also shows up as discomfort with feminine mannerisms from a man or a woman. People negatively perceive feminine style and behaviors.

A woman's status can be raised if she acts or appears more masculine. A man's status, however, lowers if he is perceived as feminine. In an episode of the 1990's television show Seinfeld, George Costanza, played by Jason Alexander, bought a pair of prescription glasses. George was the epitome of the non-starter character. He moved from job to job, sometimes had to move in with his parents, and failed at relationships. In the "Lady Glasses" episode, George's friends suspected and then confirmed that George bought and was wearing women's prescription glasses. Only a flop like George would wear women's glasses or otherwise behave in a way that is feminine. And yet, it's okay many times in our culture for women to model their style after men. We often think drab colors and masculine lines in women's clothing are chic and sophisticated.

Designer Coco Chanel started the menswear movement for women, and actresses such as Katharine Hepburn, Marlene Dietrich, and Diane Keaton popularized it (Alberts 2016). In 2017, Melissa McCarthy portrayed White House Communications Director, Sean Spicer, on Saturday Night Live. Dressed otherwise as Sean Spicer, McCarthy wore Ivanka Trump pumps and a bracelet. The Washington Post reported that President Trump did not appreciate a woman portraying his Communications Director. This skit made the Director look too feminine, and therefore too weak (Izadi 2018). This was a big "no-no" for Trump's macho, strong-man administration. This pervasive contempt for the feminine in our culture, our scornful mocking of soft, creative, nurturing energy and beauty undermines balance. This balance has the potential to support success for individuals, organizations, and cultures.

YIN AND YANG

Principles of "yin-yang" teach us that conditions or forces that at first glance appear to be opposite such as masculine and feminine, are often interconnected and interdependent. To embody or personify one, we must also have the other. Shadow requires light, night requires day, internal requires external, and left requires right. We do not and cannot experience or understand one without the other. Each completes the other and provides balance. Each also contains some of the other.

This is true for feminine and masculine. Each of us has both within us. We embody both feminine and masculine energy to varying degrees and each personally need to find this unique balance within ourselves. Balance leads us to joy in life. Our teams need to find the balance, and our organizational cultures need to find the balance too to be optimally successful. Our culture can make it difficult or impossible to find and embrace the feminine energy within us.

I challenge you to make time and space for your feminine emergence in your life. Your emergence will lead you to balance and joy. And it's a continuous process.

FINDING MY WOMEN'S CIRCLE

One day, I was at my gym. I had been out of work for eight months due to a layoff and was getting my consulting practice launched. The women's locker room has a lounge with sofas and a TV. A woman sat on a sofa, and as I walked by I saw she was working on a needle craft. It looked like nothing I'd ever seen before. From my vantage point, I could see over her shoulder and had a good view of what she was working on. I glanced as I passed. I backed up, I looked again. I started to walk forward but felt I could not leave what I was looking at without finding out more. It literally was stunning to my eyes and took my breath away.

I came around to the front of the sofa, and asked, "What IS that?" I had grown up doing needlepoint, latch hook, cross stitch, and embroidery. As an adult, I've crocheted. I was unfamiliar with what she had in her lap. It had a variety of threads, and some were sparkly. There were crystals and beads, fuzz, and other textures I couldn't describe. I felt drawn to it. She said, "It's needlepoint." We introduced ourselves, and I sat next to her for a closer look. Her project was the size of a shoe box. On it was a Christmas scene complete with Santa, his sleigh, a few reindeer, snow, presents, stars, and a snow bunny. It was exquisite. I couldn't breathe.

She told me that when she was done stitching, it would be sent to a finisher to be made into either a pillow, a display for her wall or a stand-up decoration. She seemed peaceful and full of joy. She was serene. She told me she was waiting for her husband and that this is something she does when she's waiting.

I kept feeling in my heart, "I want! I Want! I WANT!" My emotions swelled. I felt tears come to my eyes. It was so stunning.

I said, "Well, I've never seen needlepoint that looks like THAT before!"

She told me where she got her supplies and where she took classes. She told me that classes are essential and having a good instructor who can help with thread and stitch choice is very important. I felt like I'd entered a parallel universe where people care about loveliness, creativity, and things that take time and attention, and where if something is as big as a shoe box, it's still worth making grand and taking time on.

I couldn't get needlepoint out of my mind. It was in my brain, and I couldn't get it out. Needlepoint. Needlepoint. Needlepoint. How had needlepoint changed so much in thirty-five years? Well, lots of things have changed I guess. I found myself searching the Internet extensively and learning about needlepoint. I learned where the shops were in Houston, I learned about hand-painted canvases and different threads, tools, and accessories. I learned of Facebook groups, needlepoint retreats, and I learned that LNS stands for local needlepoint shop.

How is it that entire industries exist without me, a relatively informed and sophisticated person, knowing about them? Well, I guess we can't know everything. But I was shocked, maybe too shocked. I felt an unusually high level of "All this is happening without ME!" which told me I needed to learn more. I was missing out on something.

As luck and the Universe would have it, there was an LNS about a quarter of a mile from my home, essentially in my backyard. Go figure. I walked in one afternoon, and there were six women sitting in there stitching. The owner greeted me and asked if I stitched. I said no, and expressed interest. She said she was teaching a class, but I was welcome to look through the store. I'd never been inside anyplace like this shop. It was lovely. The walls were covered floor to ceiling and wall to wall with stunning hand-painted needlepoint canvases. There were only women in the shop (and a meticulously coifed standard poodle named Heathcliff who I later fell in love with and had regular hug-fests with). The women sat around tables talking and doing needlepoint. Soothing music played and the light was bright but soft as each woman worked on creating something charming and personal.

As I looked around at the canvases, the women who were stitching were telling me what a great teacher their instructor was. She alternated between helping her students and checking on me and answering my questions. How do you select threads? How do you pick a canvas? Is it best to start with a smaller canvas? I was mesmerized. My soon-to-be teacher told me it's best to start with a canvas that you love. So, there it was. I was learning, or re-learning (maybe I'd known this all the time on some level) to decide based on emotions. This felt new. My M-O was to make decisions based on data, not emotions. My education in statistics and measurement served me well, but now I loved this new feeling of being guided by feelings.

After I found my canvas, Maya (the instructor) and I selected threads, and she taught me my first stitch. Now I was in the circle. I felt at home. I felt as though I belonged. It felt comfortable to sit there with these women. Maya watched me stitch and asked me if I honestly did not do needlepoint. I confirmed, she said I was talented. When you are called to an activity or experience, it flows, it feels natural. And when what is clicking in you is part of the feminine divine, it is soothing and nurturing to your soul, and that peaceful feeling may stretch beyond you.

My canvas, for you needle pointers, was a Maggie. It was a picture of a butterfly landing on a flower. I was experiencing transformation, and I wanted to express that and live it in the art I was starting. I am close to finishing that piece. I've started and finished others in the meantime. My butterfly is breathtaking. I've used fine threads, ribbons, elaborate Swarovski crystals and other embellishments. I almost don't want to finish the butterfly because I enjoy working on it so much. When I am done with it, I want to frame it and put it some place where I will see it every day, maybe in my office.

Something extraordinary happens when creative women sit in a circle. There is an energy that is unmistakable. Over the last few years, I've made dear friends among these needle pointers. These women are of varied ages and from diverse backgrounds. They come to take part because it is artistic and relaxing. It is a special place to create and bond. It is a flow activity. When I stitch, it is immediately relaxing, I feel the tension release from my body and I know I'm in a state of feminine energy. This is the passive, receptive, creative mode.

I encourage everyone to have an activity like this in their lives. Some of my clients and friends enjoy yoga, walking, painting, or quilting for the same reasons. I recommend that everyone meditates. We need this open space and relaxed time for our brains and spirits. Needlepoint can act as a mantra for me. When I count my stitches, "over one, over two, over three; over one, over two, over three; over one, over two," and so on, it feels like meditating to a mantra.

A few of my friends tease me about doing needlepoint. They say, "What are you stitching, Grandma?" and I just laugh and ignore it. There is a stereotype about needlepoint that it's for old ladies. I also think this mocking stems from the disdain in our culture for feminine activities and energy. In needlepoint groups you'll see women of all ages, backgrounds, ethnicities, economic statuses, and fashion styles. I only mention this because you might consider an activity and feel held back because you think you might not fit in with the participants. Go check it out. You never know.

If you feel a powerful "I want! I Want! I WANT!" in your heart, listen. You never know. It could be a call from your soul to start something that will give you great joy and satisfaction. Go. Check. It. Out. It might be the divine feminine reaching out to you and tapping you on the shoulder to deliver you a dose of joy. I found a niche that fed the feminine part of me and created more balance and joy in my life. I recommend every person, family, team, and organization does the same.

66

INTEGRATE FEMININE AND MASCULINE ENERGIES.
THIS MAKES ROOM FOR SUCCESS AND JOY.
EMBRACE YOUR FEMININE ENERGY!
—Lisa Liszcz

7

Tipping Point

CHAPTER 7

Our culture is changing. Women are speaking up. Men and women are operating more from a divine feminine energy and finding their power in this energy. We are stepping into this power. We are witnessing a tipping point. Four seminal events tipped the seesaw:

- Women rose to mid-level power in numerous industries over the last decade.
- Many credible women accused Bill Cosby of sexual assault in 2016, and the courts took the allegations seriously.
- Hillary Clinton ran a sound and effective campaign for president as a qualified and talented candidate, and an unqualified, limited man won the election instead of her.
- Women and men marched in record numbers to support feminine issues in January 2017.

…and the tide turned.

Throughout 2017, powerful men lost their jobs or became embroiled in lawsuits, and people asked, "What is happening?" At dinner one night with five friends, we were talking about more men in the news losing their jobs.

As the waiter opened our wine, he said, "Soon, no one will have a job!"

We all laughed, but what was happening was amazing and overwhelming. The names on the lists occasionally shocked me, as when respective networks fired Garrison Keillor and Charlie Rose based on harassment charges. I felt sadness, and so much disappointment for the women and the men affected. Although I'd studied women's issues and worked with women for decades and experienced sexual harassment myself, the scope and depth of daily news stories depressed even me.

Many women held mid-level positions. Women enjoyed more public credibility and value to their companies than ever before. They had gravitas. They came forward, and people listened to them. I heard people say women such as Gretchen Carlson, Megyn Kelly, Ashley Judd, Gwyneth Paltrow and Angelina Jolie put nothing at risk by coming forward, and that the real heroes are women who come forward and then lose their jobs. Yes, I understand that a woman who just started working at Uber and reports sexual harassment faces retaliation or firing, showing tremendous bravery.

We must remember that women like Carlson, Kelly and the others listed have enough clout and credibility in their respective professions to be taken seriously when accusations of this magnitude are made. These women and the other public figures who brought their stories forward were not looking for attention, they already received attention and opportunities because of their prestigious careers and name recognition. *They came forward to protect other women.*

These selfless acts of bravery exemplify the "What can I do? How can I help?" collaborative, egoless spirit that is feminine. It is not self-preserving or self-promoting, it is about "How can I be part of the change?" We had our critical mass. Anita Hill helped us define the problem. The critical mass demanded change and would settle for nothing less.

Similarly, in the case of Bill Cosby in 2016, over sixty women accused Cosby of sexual assault or harassment. This large force of women and the similarity of their stories made the case compelling. We could not disregard such a large number of women. They had varied backgrounds and similar stories. They seemed credible. Their strength was in their numbers and their collaboration.

These women did not have fame or huge fortune, they had compassion for potential future victims, they had empathy and conscience which they followed. Cosby's 2017 trial ended in mistrial. In 2018, the court convicted Cosby on three counts of assault. His sentencing is scheduled for later this year, but justice has been served.

On the other hand, people who wanted Hillary Clinton to win the 2016 Presidential Election felt robbed. She lost for several valid reasons. Many of us understood that at least part of the reason she lost was due to latent and pervasive misogyny. The election had been ugly and damaging. The Internet swam with jokes and degrading, disparaging comments referring to Hillary day after day. Many of these comments were personal and reeked of misogyny. According to sociologist, Allan G. Johnson, "Misogyny is a cultural attitude of hatred for females because they are female" (Johnson 2000). Johnson says misogyny manifests in many ways, from jokes to pornography, violence, to the contempt women may be taught to feel toward themselves.

It interested me that during the campaign, people wrote vitriolic comments on social media concerning Hillary Clinton and Melania Trump. Comments on Donald Trump in social media were not as personal and biting. We criticize women more easily than we criticize men, and we are more personal with it. Women tend to be more self-deprecating and suffer more from low self-esteem. In the U.S., we don't think of women as equal to men. We think of them as "less than" or "other," not equal. Not as good as.

To paraphrase my neighbor, leaders need to be men; it's tradition. To quote my mother, "Boys are better than girls." (I'll write more on this in Chapter 8.) And as a few women told me, a lot of people couldn't stand her voice... a woman's voice.

We don't pay and promote women equally.
We don't have an Equal Rights Amendment.
Women are not equal in this country. The election reminded us.

Disappointment unfolded into activism. The energy among Hillary supporters and people who felt we were moving in the wrong direction in our country embraced the same spirit of, "What can I do? How can I help?" that grew in 2016. The fierce boldness that motivates women and men to build coalitions and act bubbled up. It was not just me. Generations of women felt long-held frustrations bubbling up. We couldn't hold it down. The energy of the mama wolf protecting her cubs showed up as, "I can no longer count on my President to protect children or the environment, so I better get involved. I better protect children more and protect the environment more than I have before."

We thought there might be others like us, who felt the same as we did, and wanted the same things and will act. We found each other on January 21, 2017, when we marched all over the world. Roughly five million people marched in U.S. cities, and more marched internationally. Our insight regarding the power of our strength in numbers with peaceful messaging and collaboration grew. This activism modeled organic, fertile, integrated, collaborative, wise, measured, and inspired action. The impact took my breath away. I was without words as I watched media coverage for the next few days. Momentum grew. I felt energized and proud. I wondered, "Is something changing? Even though we couldn't elect a woman for president?"

The pump was primed, and in 2017 the water flowed. Publicly, over eighty-four women came forward to accuse Harvey Weinstein of Miramar films and The Weinstein Company of sexual harassment and assault. Over fifty more male public figures were accused of sexual harassment and/or assault in 2017. Many of these accusations were corroborated multiple times, and most times the men accused paid for their behavior either personally, professionally or both.

Survivors of sexual harassment and assault carry irreparable harm in their souls in the form of shame and damaged self-esteem. A group of these survivors, named The Silence Breakers, received Time Magazine's 2017 "Person of the Year" award (Zachary, Dockterman, and Edwards 2017). I loved that. I can't tell you how many times I've stayed quiet regarding violations of my space, dignity or self-esteem in the workplace, or how many times I've coached women through similar processes. It is so very difficult to speak up and defend yourself. I've been challenged, questioned, and threatened when I've spoken up. It's a daunting experience. Personally, I felt very alone. In 2017, victims had sisters they could reach out to and lean on, voices lifted in unity to make a change.

In response to speaking up for myself when I've been violated, I have been told I do not have a sense of humor, that I imagined things, or I overreacted. Some companies and their leaders imply, or believe there exists, no such thing as a horny predator in corporate America. They surmise that if someone is accused, the accuser must've imagined the violation or exaggerated the circumstances.

I have been told I need to get used to the state of affairs because, "That is the way things are here."

I have been told that if I want to fit in, I will go along and not, "rock the boat," or make trouble for anyone.

These responses suggest, "We enjoy and protect our predators here." These behaviors and attitudes send the message to women, "After all, boys will be boys, and you don't matter. We hired/promoted you because of EEOC requirements." That is old-school, outdated thinking. It is wrong, and it's going away. Fewer men and women will tolerate this thinking or action today.

While watching cases surface in the news last year, my heart burst with pride. These women, all the silence breakers, were tough as nails. They were not coming forward for themselves. Many of them had been out of their salacious circumstances for years. Many were not in contact with their harassers or assaulters anymore. They came forward because they were following their consciences and wanted to protect others. They wanted to tell the truth.

These actions exemplify functioning from feminine energy, and we need more of it in our businesses and our country. This is egoless, generous action. Once again they had the numbers, large numbers of women came forward day after day, week after week. There were a few at first, and then more women spoke out. The mutual support, the collaboration that showed up among women who shared their painful stories, inspired the growth of more strength so that others could come forward too.

And the movement built. It snowballed. People talked about assault, harassment and rape, punitive behavior, sexism, and misogyny. It was like a boil opened up for cleansing, purification, and healing. A stench reeked from the pervasive, predatory behavior and the obvious systemic webs of deceit and enablement as these stories continued to expose themselves and the true characters of some powerful men were exposed. Collectively, hundreds of strong survivors (mostly women and a few men) shone a light on dark secrets they had kept for decades.

The snowball grew beyond Hollywood, Washington DC and New York and expanded out into the #MeToo movement. Long used by social activist, Tarana Burke, and publicized on social media by Alyssa Milano in 2017, women and men used #MeToo to acknowledge that they too had experienced sexual harassment or assault (Langone 2018). Again, famous women like Reese Witherspoon, Ellen DeGeneres, and Simone Biles got involved and bolstered visibility and awareness for the hashtag. When Alyssa Milano first tweeted the phrase "Me too" around noon on October 15, 2017, the supporters tweeted the phrase or hashtag over 500,000 times by the next day. On Facebook alone, the hashtag was used by over 4.7 million people in 12 million posts during the first twenty-four hours. It blew up. Women and men all over the world used the hashtag.

Every woman I've ever worked with has experienced some level of sexual harassment or assault during her career. I have. I took part in the #MeToo tweet-fest. It felt surreal. We finally talked of what no one ever talked of. Survivors shared their stories from all industries near and far. They exposed their vulnerability, and through everyone's stories we all found strength and went to our, "What can I do? How can I help?" questions. We wanted to act. There were so many of us.

Women's pent-up frustration with misogyny opened up and delivered a tipping point in 2017. Women coming forward in cases such as Cosby and O'Reilly, and sexual harassment and sexual assault cases in 2016, built momentum for the tipping point. The 2016 election and continued sexual harassment charges stories in the news built energy in the feminine emergence movement. The synergy and power of these events tipped the scales. Thus, as we've discussed, the tipping point of 2017 began, with the Women's March in January, a global event in response to Trump's election and his inauguration on January 20.

In late 2017, a sexual harassment problem in the entertainment business became world news. Powerful women pulled together to form and sponsor a movement called "Time's Up" (Langone 2018). These women wanted to create solutions for women in the entertainment industry and beyond who do not have the power, control, and resources they had. With regular meetings that deepened the bond among them, 300 actresses and female agents, writers, directors, producers and entertainment executives partnered with legal advisors to form Time's Up. They backed Time's Up with over $13,000,000. Now they work with women who are, for example, janitors, nurses, and workers at farms, factories, restaurants and hotels.

Time's Up helps women protect themselves from sexual harassment or assault, or retaliation from reporting it. The phrase "Time's Up" became a popular hashtag and slogan celebrating change. This movement embodies innovation and strength based on compassionate principles. As a leaderless movement, Time's Up members work together as partners, and the women in Time's Up report feeling supported. They enjoy deepening their female relationships and making a positive change in the world. How truly feminine.

Merriam-Webster's Dictionary defines a tipping point as, "The critical point in a situation, process, or system beyond which a significant and often unstoppable effect or change takes place." (Merriam-Webster Inc. 2016). A tipping point is when we've had enough, and we go to the other side - the level of pain that change requires no longer outweighs the pain of keeping the status quo. We are ready for a change. A tipping point happens at an individual, group, or macro level.

An example of a macro level change happens when a society or culture is ready for a change. Then the change flows. No one can stop it. It is as though someone put weights on a seesaw and tipped the seesaw. At a key point in adding weights to the high side of the seesaw, the tipping point, the seesaw must go to the other side. There is no holding it back. It must tip, and it tips easily. It is the same with a balance scale. When you put enough weight on one side, it is going to tip.

Here, there was enough weight on one side. Using the metaphor, there was enough weight (women and men speaking up) to tip the scale or the seesaw. It is the removal of tolerance on the side that has been held down. Imagine a seesaw. On one side, holding that side of the seesaw down, historically, we piled up cover-ups, complicity, silence, and tolerance of abuse. We looked the other way, and there was nothing on the other side of the seesaw. In 2017, we stacked, one-by-one on the other side of the seesaw, speaking up, boldness, defiance, bravery, honesty, determination and the #MeToo movement. The seesaw tipped.

We've seen other tipping points in our time. When people realized that personal computers were not a luxury but a necessary business and educational tool, that was a tipping point. Once we got on the personal computer bandwagon, momentum built. There was no going back. This will be the same. There will be no turning back.

66

WHEN WE CREATE ENOUGH ENERGY,
WE REALIZE A TIPPING POINT.
WE ARE EXPERIENCING A TIPPING POINT OF
FEMININE EMERGENCE.
—Lisa Liszcz

8

My Story

CHAPTER 8

I watched and waited for decades for the next wave of Feminism to start. I looked forward to feminine emergence and wondered if it would ever come while I hoped for a future where girls would be valued the same as boys.

I want all girls to value ourselves and each other, because I know how painful it is to live and not feel valued. I grew up with a mother who told me, "Boys are better, they just are." She told me that men are stronger, smarter, better leaders, and overall more impressive than women. To that end, she gave my brother special treatment around cars, allowance, and curfews while we grew up. Some might say she spoiled him. When my sister and I asked my mother why my brother, who was the baby, got special privileges, Mom would say, "because he's a boy," and smile. We were supposed to accept that as a valid explanation. My brother did not even have chores around the house, like my sister and I did. My sister mowed our grass.

MY BIRTHDAY

As a young girl, my mother told me on my birthdays the story of the day she had me. It was November 21, 1963 and Mom was twenty-five years old. She said that in those days (the 1960s), women spent a week in the hospital after having a baby. Mom thought that was wonderful that she got a week of help and rest when she had her first two children, me and my older sister, Robbin. Mothers also did not learn the sex of their baby until the baby was born.

Mom said, "In those days, we [pregnant women] got anesthesia when we had a baby. They knocked us out. We slept through the whole thing. When we woke up, the nurse handed the new mom a cleaned, swaddled baby." She said after she gave birth to me, the nurse came in with a baby — me — swaddled in pink.

The nurse said, "Hello, Mrs. Liszcz. Congratulations! You have a baby girl."

Mom would pound her fist on something nearby (a table or her thigh) and tell me she wanted to say to the nurse, "God dammit!" because she did not want a girl. She wanted a boy. She already had a girl. She hoped and prayed to have a boy. My mother wanted a girl and a boy, that is all — no more children. She thought two would be perfect. Honestly, I'm not certain she wanted any. Believing it was a woman's duty to have children, two was her limit.

Mom told me that at that moment when she learned she'd conceived and produced a second daughter, she became livid. She understood circumstances would require her to have another child. Mom said my father, an only child, wanted a son to carry on his family name. As an adult, I asked my father and he told me that he expressed no such expectations. I'm not sure what is true. I regretted being born and causing my mother pain. It hurt me that she didn't want me. I spent a lot of my life trying to make it up to her and myself.

In my coaching practice, I talk with women clients who have similar stories and who sense being unwanted by their parents because of their gender. I also know clients, and have talked with women socially, who share with me that in their family systems they simply are not as valued as their brothers. Even if the brother is estranged, in trouble with the law, or a social dropout, parents still rely more heavily on their sons for help, advice, company, and support. Mothers particularly seem to prefer the counsel and presence of sons over daughters. I've heard and experienced myself over and over again how holidays, birthdays, Mother's Days or Father's Days are not special unless the son is there.

My mother simply could not enjoy a holiday unless my brother, Todd, came. She would be grumpy and irritable. I remembered a Thanksgiving in 1998. I talked to my mother on the phone a few weeks before Thanksgiving, and she moaned and groaned about being lonely and bored. She said she wished she had plans for Thanksgiving. I invited her to my house to enjoy our dinner with us, it would be a traditional dinner with a few unique dishes added. My first husband and I liked to cook, and we always made a wonderful Thanksgiving dinner. We would have friends over, and my husband's kids would come over. It would be fun.

She stalled a bit, then she talked about other things. My brother, God love him, did not entertain or even cook. Finally, I pushed her and said, "Well, are you coming or not?"

"No. I don't want to come to your house. I want to have Thanksgiving with Todd!" she seethed. I told her good luck with that. Mom did have Thanksgiving dinner with Todd that year. She took him to a steakhouse, and she paid the bill. Mom would do anything for him. She adored him and loved being with him.

Sometimes, Mom visited Robbin's house for holiday dinners. Robbin always said Mom just grumbled and criticized the food, she refused to be happy unless Todd was next to her. Usually, she bitched at and criticized him. Still, she wanted him with her. As my mother faded away from this earth while in hospice care during 2016, she wanted Todd next to her. She would call for him for no reason. Or she would ask him something nonsensical such as, "Move that picture one inch for me," or "Where is the remote?" when the remote rested next to her hand. She would call for Todd even when Robbin or a nurse was physically closer, just to get him near her. The love of her life, she existed for him. She was forever intensely happy and proud that she put a son on this earth.

COLLEGE GIRL

When I talked about going to college, Mom angrily disagreed.

"College is for boys. Girls only go to college to get their 'M. R. S. degrees.' If you go to college, you'll become too masculine, and boys will not like you. Lesbians go to college. The only women who get degrees are teachers and nurses. They make little money anyway, so just be a secretary," she said.

She told me she and her fourth husband (my stepfather) Melvin, would not pay for it. My father took the role of an absentee parent shortly after my parents' divorce, when I was six years old. I planned to go to a junior college in town. I saw it as my only option. I did not know how to apply anywhere else or how I would pay for living expenses. I earned exceptional grades in high school and automatically qualified to go to a few state schools, but I was clueless about how to sign up without a parent's permission. I had no one to help me. Melvin said he would pay the tuition, but we needed to keep that between him and me. Mom gave me no support, emotional or otherwise.

Melvin worked for an oilfield pipeline company in Houston. They sponsored a great program for employees in the '70s. As a dependent of an employee, when I enrolled to go to college in the fall, Melvin's company hired me for the summer. I got a secretary job working for a VP of something or other because I'd enrolled to go to San Jacinto College, South Campus in the Fall. I'd picked Psychology as my major. I'd been an artist in high school, but I did not think I could make much money doing that, so I signed up for Psychology speculating I might be a Psychologist someday. I'd met one woman therapist while in high school, and I found her interesting and spiritual. The idea of helping people appealed to me.

That secretary's job bored me to tears. About once a week someone came into the office, and twice a month I needed to type a letter. Maybe four times a week the phone rang. Basically, I sat and waited all week. I made $4.25 an hour. That exceeded minimum wage by 90 cents an hour, so I was "rolling in the dough," so to speak. I made good money for sitting and waiting that summer. My mother concluded I had hit THE BIG TIME. I had everything she valued in a job for a woman. I dressed up to go to work, according to her I made great money, and I worked for a man with a big job title and a lot of responsibility. My job consisted of everything she could imagine a girl could want, so she could not imagine why I continued to plan to go to college.

During my first year of college, our relationship deteriorated. She wanted me to marry my high school boyfriend, stay in Friendswood, work as a secretary, and have babies. When I broke up with my high school boyfriend, she stopped talking to me. I had dated him for five years and just started my third year of college. I wanted more than that relationship offered, a bigger life, and I wanted adventure. I began contemplating graduate school. I blossomed, meeting lots of new people provided so much fun, learning and getting exposed to people from different places. It was a great time for me.

I felt stuck with John. John seemed "small town." I started getting very interested in health and fitness, and John was uninterested. He told me that he resented the time I spent exercising, thirty to forty-five minutes a day. He also told me my ass was starting to look like a man's ass. That hurt my feelings. Increasingly, I enjoyed literature, philosophy and women's studies, and he did not. We grew apart. Eventually, I was not even attracted to him anymore. I broke up with him.

He got mean about the break-up, and he said horrible, vulgar things to me. He insulted me viciously. My mother, furious about the breakup, stopped talking to me. She gave me the silent treatment when I needed her support the most. She wanted me married and wanted me to be a small-town girl. I wanted more. She would not even look at me. She withdrew from me as punishment for me not being what she wanted me to be.

I looked for additional work to help pay my bills. I already worked in the Dean's office at the college in the evening, and applied for additional part-time jobs. When the phone rang at home, Mom would not give me the phone or give me my messages. She would tell the caller I wasn't there. I possessed no way of knowing if someone called me about a job interview or an offer. She sabotaged my job hunt. She wanted nothing to be easy for me, and she would not help me.

Besides me, four other people lived in the house — Mom, Melvin, my little sister Jennifer, and Todd. When mom cooked dinner, which she did every night and I give her a lot of credit for this, she would cook for four. She cooked four baked potatoes and four chicken breasts, or she cooked four corn on the cobs and four hamburgers. My mother acted like I did not exist. She would not look at me, talk to me, or acknowledge me in any way. She ostracized me because I broke up with a boy.

I started dating a fellow student named Tony. Tony came from Connecticut, studied pre-law and was Italian. Mom just loved Italians! Born and raised in Rhode Island, Mom insisted that New England was truly God's country. In Mom's opinion, anyone born outside of New England was low class and uncouth. Tony, in Mom's mind, would be a perfect addition to our family. She wanted to have him over for dinner immediately.

Needless to say, I was back in the "in-group" of Mom's team because she liked that I was dating, and she liked who I was dating. She planned to cook an Italian dinner of spaghetti and meatballs. She made delicious spaghetti and meatballs, and Tony came over for dinner. Mom worked so hard on that dinner. We ate at the formal dining room table on the good china and Mom got all dressed up and put on makeup and nice jewelry. When Tony got to our house, Mom — excited as a schoolgirl — chatted, smiled, and giggled. She flirted with Tony, batting her eyelashes at him and laughing at his jokes.

She embarrassed me. She acted like he was there to see her, like he was dating her. When Tony and I talked about it the next day he told me that he felt awkward with my mother. He talked about how some women when they get older (Mom was forty-three or forty-four) didn't get much attention. Tony sensed Mom craved male attention. It embarrassed me even more that someone saw how needy and immature my mother was. His insights and comments validated my perceptions of her.

Tony attended school in Houston for one semester. We connected and had a lot of fun together. We experienced great chemistry, and I loved being around him. He was masculine, fit, smart, and enjoyed books, culture and adventures. I delighted in dating him. Before Tony left, we agreed to have a long-distance relationship. He said he would visit again in a couple of months and that we could write letters and have phone calls. In the first letter he sent, he outlined lies he had told, and told me the truth.

I give him credit now for being honest. Tony did not leave Houston when he told me he did. He stayed an extra few days and drove to Galveston to visit a woman he dated before he dated me. At the end of his letter, he broke up with me. He said it would never work. It devastated me. That letter hurt me to the core. I never had my heart broken so badly before, I struggled to function. My mother reacted by treating me like she treated me when I broke up with my high school boyfriend, only worse.

Mom returned to not looking at me, not cooking for me, and not giving me phone messages. The tension in the house grew thick. She told Melvin to not pay attention to me too, and told him not to help me in any way. Melvin still helped me a little bit, but he had to be sneaky. He could loan me his gas card and let me put gas in my car without her knowing, and he let me use health insurance when I needed to go to the doctor. In those days, like today, an employee's dependent, which I was, could use health insurance as long as she/he was a college student, like me.

My mother told Melvin not to pay for any of my tuition or books anymore, or to give me any spending money for food. Her youngest child, Jennifer, is Melvin's. My mother threatened Melvin, saying that if she caught him helping me in any way, she would divorce him and take Jennifer away from him. Melvin took risks to help me. I had to make my way.

During final exams of our 1984 spring semester, my friend, Edna, and I started moving into our apartment. I worked several part-time jobs and went to school full-time. Every day I drove to my mother's house and packed for about an hour. I took what I packed to the apartment and dropped it off. Then I took a test or studied. I rushed, and I was stressed out. One day on one of my "pack-up-as-much-stuff-as-you-can-get-in-the-Volkswagen-Rabbit" trips between final exams and studying, Mom came into my room.

After months of avoiding me completely, she approached me and looked at me square in the eye. She held out her hand, palm up and said, "Take whatever you're going to take. Give me your key to this house. You are never coming back."

I dug in my purse and found my keychain. I removed my house key and put it in her palm. She closed her hand and walked out of the bedroom. I was on my own at twenty. With fifteen minutes before I needed to leave for my next final exam, I grabbed clothes, purses, shoes, and jewelry. I took high school graduation mementos, a few pictures and gifts from my Polish grandmother. Snapping up what I could, I threw everything into my car. I drove to college with my stuff in my car, and I took an exam. It was sociology. I did well.

I began to hate my mother. I hated everything about her, her big ass, how much she drank and smoked, the nasty chicken skin on her arms and legs, her long, claw-like fingernails, and her jowly face. I began to hate her softness and her vulnerability. I started to hate how feminine she could be, and I internalized all of it on myself.

I wanted to be tough and strong. I hated that she valued her femininity. She most highly valued her ability to catch a man. Mom never failed to attract who she wanted, and she was married to her fourth husband. My mother had always been pretty and stylish. She liked pretty things and romantic stories and soap operas. In rebellion, I embraced all my masculine energy around mental activity, fitness, earning money, telling and doing.

She chose to define me based on my ability to attract and keep a man. How successful, attractive, and "well-bred" that man was also defined me. At mid-life, she still considered herself the "belle of the ball," and she wanted to show me how to be one too, if only I would pay attention and learn. She may not have even known what she was doing, it all seemed unconscious.

I began to reject everything feminine as silly and unimportant. I exercised until my body became muscular and lean. My body fat dropped so much that my menstrual cycle stopped and I menstruated intermittently for most of my college years. Focused on action, science, data, and logic, I embraced feminism as a way to change the world by being strong. In college, I focused on large, worldly and sophisticated issues. I met new people, dated and made new friends. I learned about new ideas and concepts. I could not get enough. My focus was external and not so much internal. As I buried everything feminine deep inside of me, I planted seeds for my personal feminine emergence later.

Life was tough when I lived with Edna. I worked four jobs to make money to support myself, but that was not enough. I took out student loans. My sister and brother-in-law gave me a mattress that laid on the floor and a comforter, and I bought a set of sheets. Edna and I acquired a phone, TV, and a couch. We shared a bathroom. Edna didn't pay her share of the bills on time, which made things even tougher on me.

We split after our six-month lease expired, and I got my place. By then, I worked six jobs and cash flow got slightly better. I taught aerobics classes at three different locations, worked the front desk at a fitness facility, wrote a weekly article for a newspaper, and worked as a weekend receptionist for a yacht brokerage. I held those jobs for a little over a year, then I received more money in student loans and I quit the weekend job. It was still tough, but I enjoyed having my place.

I leased a one-bedroom apartment, bought, found or received donated furniture, and got a queen size bed. I was still a virgin. When I had sex for the first time at twenty-one years old, it was in my apartment in my bed that I bought. My "first" was a sweet guy, and he knew that he was my first. I was emotionally strong about it. I remember talking with my friend, Jan, who supported me and was very kind. I wish I had a supportive and caring mother or sister to talk with. I wish I had more loving female support in my life, such as a fun aunt or older female cousin. But I didn't. Again, I felt confident and good about myself, but I was alone.

WHAT MELVIN SAID

My first two years of college, I went to a local junior college, San Jacinto College, South Campus. Melvin paid for my tuition and books and helped me with gasoline money. I paid for my car insurance and all other expenses. As I've said, my mother was vehemently opposed to my attending college. She told me, "Lisa, it's a man's world. It makes no sense for a woman to go to college. Just get along being a secretary or a receptionist. That's a woman's role in a man's world."

One day when I still lived in her house, I overheard her telling my grandmother (her mother) that she had been discussing my going to college with Melvin. Melvin and I had a good relationship. He married my mother when I was about thirteen. He was (and still is) a sensitive man who listened to me and gave me advice when I was a teenager. Melvin parented me more than either one of my natural parents. I appreciated him and loved him a lot.

I heard my mother tell my grandmother that she talked to Melvin about my going to college and how concerned she was. She wanted me to get married and settle down. Mom wanted me to marry my high school boyfriend who I was still dating at the time, she did not understand my desire to venture into "a man's world." My mother told my grandmother that Melvin reassured her and told her not to worry about it, that I would never finish college. I heard her say, "Melvin said, 'She'll never finish. She'll get hot pants for some guy and drop out. They all do.'"

Hot pants? What the fuck? I felt as though someone had punched me in the gut. I felt betrayed by the one parent figure I had in my life. Even Melvin did not understand my passion for education, my focus, and my ambition. I had no one who believed in me. Did Melvin really say that? I don't know, we never spoke of it. At seventeen years old, it was a devastating blow that unleashed in me an even stronger determination to be strong, independent, and driven. I buried everything feminine within me as deeply as I could. That is what many men and women do.

I've shared personal stories with you because my personal stories are not unique. While they seemed unique at the time I experienced them, they are fairly universal. Details differ, but most professional women (and men) I've spoken with over the last two decades also suppressed their feminine energy, consciously or unconsciously. We see feminine energy mocked and otherwise devalued in our culture, and while young we learn to suppress it. A young boy skipping is told to stop because he looks too "girly." A teenage girl playing sports cries over a loss and her coach tells her to, "toughen up" because we don't cry in sports.

Our masculine culture teaches us to distrust feelings and intuition, two of our most powerful guidance systems. I recommend a different strategy for a full, joyful life.

"

MISOGYNY IS TAUGHT WHEN WE ARE YOUNG.
AS ADULTS, IF WE EMBRACE
FEMININE EMERGENCE WE CAN
FIND JOY AND PEACE.
—Lisa Liszcz

9

What To Do With Feminine Energy

CHAPTER 9

As women and men, what should we do with our feminine energy?

EMBRACE IT!!! EXPRESS IT!!!

The world needs your feminine energy, and so do you. No matter your age or situation, start finding ways now to embrace and express your feminine energy every day.

As discussed in Chapters 3 and 4, our culture does not celebrate and encourage the divine feminine. I learned to suppress my feminine energy and got rewarded for that in most of my personal and professional life. At what cost - to me, those close to me, and to the companies I worked for? Significant cost. I've learned valuable lessons from my experience and from talking with other strong, smart women about their experiences with feminine and masculine energy.

Usually, we do not realize the cost of feminine energy suppression until midlife or until a crisis such as an illness, loss of a loved one, or loss of a job. Then life forces us to wake up from our fog and face that something that's missing from our lives, something authentic and true.

Joy is missing from our lives; meaning, purpose, intimacy, emotion, and self-expression are missing. When we live life primarily engaged in masculine energy, we rob ourselves and those around us of these innate human gifts.

How do we get it back? Embrace feminine energy and build the appropriate balance back into your life. I will tell you how. First, I will share with you stories from the women I interviewed. They gave amazing insights.

THE INTERVIEWS

During summer 2016, I interviewed forty-four professional women about mid-career and midlife issues. We discussed personal transformation, happiness, well-being, career change, and finding meaning and purpose. I collected information and perspectives on these topics that my clients and I often discuss. The women I interviewed lived mostly in the United States, with a small number living in Canada, United Arab Emirates, Scotland, China, and Russia. They ranged in age from thirty-one to sixty-three, with an average age of forty-nine, and worked in finance, oil and gas, chemical manufacturing, education, law, and not-for-profit fields. I interviewed business owners, professionals, and executives in human resources and finance, sales and marketing professionals, engineers, C-suite executives, consultants, and more.

I asked each of the women for twenty minutes, but most of my interviews lasted for an hour. A few went even longer. These generous women shared honest stories and insights. I found our conversations to be heartfelt and touching.

HELPING OTHERS

Most of the women had a strong desire to help others. They wanted to mentor professional women, volunteer with elder care or with animals, or commit time to help with other causes. They said they were always too busy to "give back" as much as they wanted. Their corporate jobs and responsibilities kept them overwhelmed with business. The busy, action-oriented lives they described were masculine. They expressed strong desires to be in situations where they could empathize with and nurture others, this was feminine. They longed for opportunities to give in this way. They were out of balance.

One woman shared that she looked forward to doing volunteer work after she retired. Another woman told me that sometimes she fantasized about quitting her big corporate job and being a greeter at Walmart where she could make people smile and feel comfortable. Another woman stated emphatically, "I don't know if I'm going to work with dogs or old people, but I want to take care of something!"

We all have a human need to care for or help others. The need is stronger in some of us than in others, but the need is universal, it is human. If you get this urge, I encourage you to explore and fulfill it. This is one way to embrace and express your feminine energy and allow her to emerge.

Yes, in a life bursting at the seams with "to do" lists, it's hard (or impossible) to fit one more thing in. I hear you. I learned from the interviews that when we do not prioritize what is critical for our joy, we live empty lives full of regrets.

Ask your Inner Wise Woman, your Inner Divine Feminine (I don't care if you're a man, woman, bi-sexual, transsexual, questioning, or other), what brings you joy. Write these "to do's" at the top of your list. If "helping others" and "giving back" show up at the top of your list, prioritize these activities, as they will feed your soul and bring you joy and energy. They will also lead you to an authentic life.

RELATIONSHIPS

The women I interviewed craved intimate relationships. They wanted women friendships, intimate partners, and people in their lives they could confide in, travel and have fun with. With demanding careers (and some raised children), they had not made time for relationships. Marriages became distant. Some were not married or in significant relationships. Most missed having friendships. They were lonely.

One woman told me that she loved to travel but didn't anymore. She was tired of group tours; she had done so many. Without a partner to travel with, it was not fun for her anymore. Another woman told me that she and her husband of over twenty years lived separate lives. Her goal was to work on that relationship, but she did not sound hopeful. Another woman told me that she missed having girlfriends as she had in high school and college. It was difficult to bond with other women at work due to competition and politics, and outside of work, she didn't have time.

The women who prioritized relationships were glad they did. They said relationships were something they consciously decided to work on and prioritize years ago, and that they knew they benefited from these intimate bonds. Relationships require work, energy, empathy and caring. They take time to blossom and grow. Researchers have documented the importance of social connection in happiness (Achor 2010; LeBlanc 2008). When we strive to "go it alone," be independent and a lone ranger, we are in our masculine energy. We put our happiness at risk because we get out of balance. When we commune with others and join the pack, we are in our feminine energy. Caring, listening, and empathizing — behaviors that build intimacy — are feminine behaviors.

Humans need social connection, some of us more than others. Many of us need more than we have. If you are missing out, I encourage you to find and build relationships. This is one way to draw on your feminine energy to bring balance, joy, and meaning to your life. It takes time and effort to build meaningful relationships. Practice helps.

INDEPENDENCE AND CREATIVITY

Interviewees expressed a longing for independence and creativity in their lives, and talked about creativity and independence together. They said they craved independence to create something fully on their own with everything they've learned in their careers or lives, and they wanted full ownership over the creative process. Women need space for self-expression in work and life (Gilligan 1993; Helson 1965, 2010). We leverage independence as a means to creativity, and creativity as a means to personal expression. Our personal expression, particularly at midlife, can be a gift to others and ourselves.

The interview participants wanted autonomy. They wanted the authority to make decisions. All were high achievers and had experienced success in male-dominated environments, they liked to do that, and it gave them energy. They still wanted to experience that energy. They did not want to give it up. But there was a new dimension to what they desired. They wanted to express their creativity, and they wanted independence over their creativity. If they were going to work on a new policy or a new program, marketing strategy or scientific innovation, they wanted control over it. I loved hearing that they wanted to be creative. I heard from them that they desired to explore a part of themselves that was dormant. They wanted to reach into that dormant place and play with it a bit to see what might happen. They wanted to spread their creative wings.

A few women told me they were interested in starting businesses. One dreamed of being an independent consultant, another woman wanted to run a winery. One interviewee ran Human Resource (HR) Departments for large companies for her career. She dreamed of starting an HR Department for a small start-up company from scratch, she wanted to put everything in place for a new company and lead the entire process. Others described similar dreams of working with small start-up companies and putting together a marketing, finance, or public relations team. Some women talked about exploring creative hobby interests that they'd put "on hold" for years. They longed to make pottery, paint, quilt, design jewelry, try creative writing or gardening. They yearned to try something new, playful, and fun.

We, humans, are creative by nature. We can't help it. It's our purpose to create and leave the world with evidence of our soul's impact. We are here to improve and elevate the world. Due to the prevalence of women's oppression in the workplace and socially, many of us do not assert ourselves in personal or professional creativity. True self-expression requires independence. Ask yourself if you have the call to create. Most of us experience joy and meaning in life through creative experiences. If you are missing out, I encourage you to prioritize creative activities. This is one way to draw on your feminine energy to bring balance, joy, and meaning to your life. You may need to cut other activities out of your day - activities that don't feed your soul.

Some of us think we are not creative — we are all creative in some way. You may have a gift for wood-working, painting murals, decoupage, photography, scrapbooking, landscape architecture, or tie-dye. Who knows? Experiment with different activities. Take classes on different topics. Focus on the pleasure of the activity, not how good or bad you are. The quality of your efforts only matters to the degree that you enjoy the experience. Your joy is what matters. Too many people, men and women, stifle their creative drives. The women I interviewed reinforced for me the importance of creative time in a joyful life.

NOT KNOWING HOW TO MOVE FORWARD

The majority of the interviewees conveyed strong desires for change in their lives. They felt stuck and stagnant. Their lives lacked the "juice" that comes from living authentically. Bored, they wanted change but did not know how to begin, what to change or what they wanted instead of what they had. They were frustrated and lost. They felt this confusion for the first time in their lives. Until mid-life, whatever was next was determined by external standards:

- Get the degree.
- Get the job.
- Get the next job.
- Get the relationship.
- Get the house.
- Get the kid(s), graduate degrees, or other.
- Get the next job.
- Get the bigger house(s).
- Get the kid(s) in college (or otherwise settled); second house; or other.
- Get the next, even better job.

...and so on.

Now, it is time to go within. In midlife, we cannot look outside of ourselves for a roadmap. We must go inside and listen to our inner voice, our intuition. This can be scary for someone who has spent decades trusting logic, data and external guidelines. It is also empowering. After burning ourselves out, we have to listen to our hearts for healing. We have to go to intuition and emotional guidance. The interviewees reported separation from their Personal Guidance Systems, also known as their intuition. Now they were being called to reconnect. They were experiencing, as I had in midlife, a strong pull to reconnect with divine feminine energy to find fulfillment and meaning.

Intuition acts as our Personal Guidance System, or PGS (Bennett 2017). Intuition guides and directs us from our inner knowing, our higher consciousness. I instruct my clients to meditate every day to activate and engage with their intuition. Like creativity and relationship building, meditating and tuning into one's PGS takes practice and time. Sometimes at first, we feel awkward practicing new things. In time, we improve and gain results. Meditation, meditative walking, and other meditative activities such as yoga, swimming, gardening, or prayer rituals facilitate our getting into a mental state conducive to hearing our inner voice. This is when we are tapped into our intuition, our PGS.

When you slow down your body, clear your mind and surrender, your intuition guides you step-by-step towards the purpose of your life. By nurturing and cultivating intuition, moving forward on change becomes much simpler. Bill Bennet, the creator of the documentary film PGS, says, "When you follow your intuition, there is no disappointment. Joy returns." You can find resources on developing intuition on my website under "Resources." We all have intuition innately available to us. We are born with it. Our intuition provides us with meaningful guidance regarding our purpose in life.

INTERVIEWS — SUMMARY

In the interviews, women told me about desiring more opportunities to help others, build relationships, and experience heightened independence and creativity. They also told me that they sometimes get stuck and are not sure what to do next. These urges are not unique to women or to the women I talked with. At midlife, creative urges and desires to give back to society surface for men and women (Brehony 1996).

These women moved me by how exhausted and disappointed many of them were, and that they did not know why. They could not think how to move forward. They did not understand their feelings. It seemed as though overdevelopment of something else had replaced natural instincts. Some of them felt lost, and yet they had everything they needed to find themselves and create the next chapter of their lives. Each one of them was fully empowered to create the life they wanted and to feel the way they wanted. It was up to them.

To build social and professional success many of us, men and women, suppress our divine feminine energy. We hide it, embracing our masculine energy at the expense of our feminine energy, sometimes for decades. Some people call this stage in life "masculine identification" or "passive acceptance" of oppression (Sage 2015; Downing and Roush 1985; Murdock 1990).

It's kind of like the Stockholm Syndrome. Someone who naturally embodies more feminine energy pushes themselves only to present masculine energy to fit in, and to be "one of the guys." This woman or man dresses, talks, behaves and even thinks in more masculine ways than their natural preferences would enable. Masculine identification leads to cutting off aspects of one's personality and spirit that lead to joy and fulfillment. It takes time to get that back. I know, because I went through it.

"

FIND WAYS EVERY DAY TO LET YOUR
FEMININE ENERGY EMERGE.
EMBRACE YOUR GENTLE SOUL AND YOUR
LOVING SPIRT.
—Lisa Liszcz

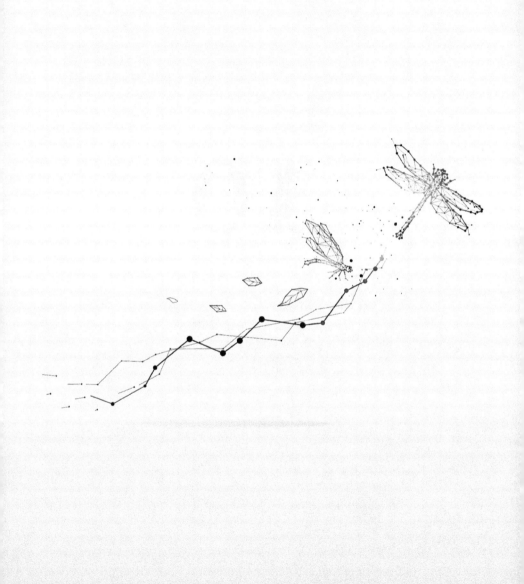

10

Masculine Identification and Little Men

CHAPTER 10

MY MASCULINE IDENTIFICATION

I blossomed in college. Away from my family, I developed my confidence. I was popular and made lots of friends. Professors liked me and nominated me for special projects and leadership roles on campus. The Women's Studies Department sponsored me on a women's student leadership conference in Virginia in my senior year, and I was thrilled to be recognized. The trip was a great experience. After being raised by a mother who'd always had a disdain for me, it was amazing to be appreciated.

College introduced my brain to the external world. I was drenched in masculine energy. I embraced action and logic, and this served me well. I consistently made honor rolls and was in honor societies. I felt driven, independent, aggressive, confident, and strong. In my situation, so alone and with essentially no family support, I could not afford vulnerability or weakness.

I was estranged from my mother and did not see her during my college years. She did not want to see me, nor I her after she kicked me out of the house. She also told my stepfather to not see me, and if he gave me any help at all she would divorce him, so he stayed away. My hatred for her grew. I rejected everything about her, her desire to be taken care of by a man, her vulnerability, her dependency on men, her enthusiastic embrace of the traditional housewife and mother role, her physical weakness and softness and her feminine style. I rejected these aspects of her and myself. I internalized my disdain for the feminine.

My mother had told me that college was not for women and that men did not like women to be too smart. For me, this contention was completely irrelevant. I could not have cared less. My brain was on fire, and I soaked up all the knowledge and information I could. I did it for myself, and I loved it. I did not care who liked or who did not like it. I loved all of it - philosophy, math, sociology, literature, statistics, every damn bit of it. I embraced all my masculine energy during college. I exercised like crazy, wore clothes that hid my figure, wore little to no makeup, and almost stopped wearing bras. I heard my mother assumed I had become a lesbian. I'm not sure, but I think she disowned me.

During the first twenty years of my career, my alignment with masculine energy continued, and it served me well. I worked in male-dominated environments, collaborated well with my male colleagues, and received regular and valuable promotions and recognition. I followed the popular professional advice of the day, wore a lot of gray and other drab colors, and wore nothing floral, colorful, or anything designed to show off my figure. I did not wear perfume, and kept my naturally curly hair smooth and under control most of the time.

I kept the tone of my voice low by speaking from my diaphragm and kept my jewelry discreet and classic. Sometimes, I bought my button-down work shirts in the boys' department at Macy's. The ones made by Ralph Lauren fit great, were cheaper than the blouses in the women's department, and they came in the drab colors and patterns I was looking for. Yes, I dressed in boys' clothes to go to work. And in those clothes, I got more respect than I would have gotten if I'd worn a colorful, flowery or polka-dotted blouse with a sweetheart neckline made by Liz Claiborne in the women's department of the same store. I'm not knocking Liz Claiborne. I bought lots of her clothes for work back then. I'm just saying that looking feminine in a manufacturing business environment in the '80s and '90s was a sure way to undermine your credibility.

During this time, I attended night school, working on my master's degree. I was married to my first husband and helped raise my two step children. I exercised four or five times a week, jogging and lifting weights. We played golf, but I did not enjoy it. I golfed for the social interaction more than the sport. I had no time for other hobbies. As a child, I liked to read, dance, draw and paint. My first husband and I planted seasonal flowers, but that was the only feminine activity I enjoyed besides helping with his teenage children. We cooked, but our cooking was very pedestrian. It was out of necessity, and we cooked low-fat, high-nutrient meals. I rarely cooked for pleasure or as a creative activity. This phase of my life was action-oriented. It was about getting things done, not about pleasure, creativity, introspection, nurturing or enjoyment. I lived a task-oriented life.

Masculine energy consumed my world starting in the early '80s. In the late '90s, I craved a change. I was in my late thirties, was finishing up my doctoral degree, and I wanted a change in my life. I went through a divorce, and I started my own company.

My new life gave me the chance to explore creativity and self-nurturing. I created new programs for client companies, marketed my company, read books on self-development, cooked for pleasure, and took dance classes. Decorating the little townhome I rented gave me a feminine retreat to rediscover my feminine energy.

My personal feminine emergence began. I burned scented candles and decorated with floral fabrics in all rooms, started going to church, met with a Jungian psychologist, and I meditated and journaled on spiritual issues. I coached clients on finding purpose in their own lives and building relationships.

I bought a new home for myself that I called my "little dollhouse." Built in the '70s, my precious home had formal entertaining areas I loved and an enclosed sunroom that looked out over a rose and azalea garden that included a rose-covered trellis. My "little dollhouse" had sweet, classic features, and I decorated it with feminine details. I ran my business out of my home for three years. This time healed a male-identification wound in me. I was energized and more balanced when I returned to a corporate role in 2004. I never bought any more shirts, or anything else, in the boys' department.

LITTLE MEN

Women make it in the business world if they are male identified. Some argue that women can male identify until they make it to the top of their profession, then they can "switch back" and female identify with their energy. Then they will have the power to help bring other women up and balance policy and aspects of corporate culture for all. Others argue that by the time someone "makes it to the top," they are unlikely to re-develop and engage strong feminine energies in a masculine environment.

Male identification happens when a woman who naturally would be stronger in feminine energy internally denounces and subjugates her feminine energy and embraces and develops masculine energy. Women make this adaptation to be successful and "fit in" in male-dominated environments. This might happen in college or business programs where women are outnumbered by men, and the culture is masculine such as in STEM programs or manufacturing businesses. Engaging in masculine energy full-time can be fun and rewarding on many levels. Over time, however, this adaptation can limit personal development, self-actualization, and happiness.

Loads of books advise women on how to be successful in the workplace. Much of this advice falls into the category I call "being a little man" advice. For women, sometimes it seems as though the organizations we work for try to turn us into "little men." Organizations hire us for our diversity, then they do not understand how to leverage the benefits of our diversity. Soon it becomes our responsibility to "fit in" or "blend in" and make others understand it's okay we're around. We take the advice in business books and cut our hair, wear drab clothes that hide our figures, and lower our voices. These adjustments help a woman fit in and give her advantages in a male-dominated workforce (Gross, Stone, and Zimbalist 2002; Molloy 1996; Frankel 2014; Heim, Hughes and Golant 2015).

It's desirable to be "one of the team." I just want to make sure that you consciously choose how far you are willing to go with your adjustments and that you do not lose yourself in the process. Check in with yourself regularly and ask, "Am I having fun with this, or is this becoming a painful sacrifice for me?" It is okay to modify your behaviors to meet your needs, this is how you take care of yourself and stay on a course of self-discovery. Just be clear about what you are doing.

When we recruit women into the workplace and then ask them to suppress their feminine energy, asking them instead to think and act like men, we are not embracing gender diversity. By asking women to magnify their masculine energy, companies keep their cultures defined by linear reasoning, competition, action orientation, analytical focus, and objectivity.

Company leaders say, "That's how things are here," and, "That's our culture." These companies miss out on rich opportunities to work with increased compassion, worldview, environmental focus, creativity, non-linear thinking, intuition and win-win solutions. In these companies, sexual harassment and discrimination continue. Everyone loses at the individual, team, and organizational levels. We lose in areas of innovation, relationship building, creativity and business growth. It can start innocently enough when we encourage women to "dress professionally," which usually means "dress more like men." Developing a balanced corporate culture takes hard work and attention.

It benefits everyone to dress conservatively in business settings. Professional attire sends a message of credibility and should not over-power your talents, skills or your message. As a woman, you want people to pay attention to you, not your clothes, jewelry, hair, makeup, or shoes. Recently, I heard a great piece of advice on business attire: Imagine what you would wear and how you would groom yourself if you were going to a nightclub and then do the opposite.

Many women and some men grow up learning that dressing themselves is an opportunity for self-expression. This is more of a feminine energy perspective than a male energy one. Picking out clothing, fixing our hair and putting on makeup can be an expression of who we are and how we are feeling on a particular day. For the people who feel this way, dressing in corporate attire can seem restrictive, boring and not fun at all. Nevertheless, it may be important to do this for the benefit of your career.

Each person needs to consciously choose for themselves how much they want to adapt this aspect of their public persona for their career. One of my clients (a woman in her late twenties) told me that she is happy to wear button-down blouses and gray suits during the week, but that she will never cut her long, beautiful red hair. She ties it back or puts it up on work days. She and her husband go dining and dancing on weekends, when she lets her hair down, literally, and wears her leather skirt and stiletto heels. That creates a fun feminine/masculine energy balance for her.

One of my male clients in his mid-career has a passion for fashion. He has reached the ultimate level in his career that he always aspired to, and the other employees and partners at his firm regard him with great respect for his distinguished career spanning over twenty years. Five years ago, he started wearing more colorful and fashionable items to work for his pleasure. The trend caught on, and the office is more fashionable now on non-client-facing days. He says morale seems better too. Wearing one special accessory just for one's pleasure, having a tattoo that no one can see, and having fashion-forward makeup for non-work times are ways that some of my clients embrace feminine energy and express their uniquenesses while respecting cultures of their conservative workplaces.

Maybe you are one of the less than 20% of women in your organization. In that case, men outnumber women by a long shot, and some may have been there for a long time - ten years or more. They remember working where you now work when there were even fewer women, and they might remember those days fondly. They might think there were fewer restrictions then, and they had more freedoms. Some of my clients describe similar organizational cultures, and I've worked in similar cultures myself. That is not your problem. You are not there to make the organization more of what it is or was. You are there to bring your talents and gifts to the organization to make it better and to make it ready for the future. Be you.

In my corporate career, I worked so hard to "fit in" that I buried an important part of myself for a long time. That left a hole in my spirit. Lost, exhausted and emotionally partitioned into my early fifties, I only came back to myself after a career crisis. A week before my 50th birthday, my employer laid me off. I'd worked there for five years. My lay off turned out to be a well-timed blessing. I am now an author, coach, speaker, and entrepreneur. So, lo-and-behold, the story that I saw nightly on the poster at my university while I was working on my doctorate came true for me, and for some of the professional women I know. And I understand why.

People say that corporate jobs suck the life out of you. But we let that happen. We let it happen because we think we deserve it, or we think it's macho, tough and admirable, wearing our fatigue and long hours worked like they are badges of courage. We choose to sacrifice ourselves and the people around us, our happiness and theirs in the name of... you guessed it... masculine priorities like competition, money, prestige, and winning.

This behavior is ego driven. We think we do not deserve to go home and have a life, be nurtured, nurture ourselves and others, so we gravitate to the jobs that will demand too much of us and give us very little in return. In corporate environments, I have seen people who will not go home at a reasonable hour. I have seen people who are in the office on weekends and who are emailing at two or three in the morning. When we do not set boundaries and prioritize ourselves, our health and our happiness, we reject our feminine instincts of compassion, nurturing and empathy. We embrace masculine energy and enjoy the rush of drive, independence, aggression, confidence, and strength. We get hooked on masculine energy and become addicted and out of balance.

It is critical that we understand that this is our choice. And we make this choice out of devaluing the... you guessed it... feminine in the world, and the feminine inside of ourselves. We have such disdain for the feminine that we will punish ourselves to prove it. The more we do this, the more we and the generations that follow us will suffer.

After getting laid off, I re-evaluated my life priorities. I knew I had to get my mind and my body healthy again. I returned to my Jungian therapist, and I participated in coaching opportunities where I reflected on my personal motivations, values, and joys in life. At fifty years old, I spent time thinking about what I wanted the next five, ten, and twenty-plus years to look like. I meditated and journaled. I wanted the next part of my life to be very intentional, and set out to grow personally, spiritually and emotionally. I set goals, wrote letters to my future self, analyzed my dreams, and started chanting and using affirmations. I was in "get-my-butt-on-the-right-track" boot camp.

I had run my own business before, for three years. Then I went to work for a client of mine. I had always missed the independent and creative work I did as an entrepreneur and business owner, so I returned to that and started doing team building workshops and professional coaching. In this work, I could engage my natural abilities around empathy, compassion, and creativity as well as my action orientation, my passion for analyzing data, and managing projects. I prioritized time with friends and family, my health, and investment in my spirituality and learning.

My life is so much more balanced and fulfilling than it was while I worked corporate jobs. And I'm healthier too, I have more energy, and I sleep better. I make time for my exercise, and I enjoy cooking and spending time with my dog, Penny, who my husband and I rescued in 2015.

I am in balance. I consciously embrace both masculine and feminine energies daily. I love playing in both energies, this stretches me and enables my authenticity.

66

ALIGN MASCULINE AND FEMININE ENERGY
WITH YOUR TRUE SELF.
BUILD AUTHENTICITY IN YOUR ENERGY FOR A
CONGRUENT LIFE.
—Lisa Liszcz

11

Integrating The Feminine into the Mainstream

CHAPTER 11

It is time to bring feminine energy into corporate cultures as part of a greater feminine emergence. It is time to accelerate the integration of feminine energy into processes and activities of organizations. With the correct balance of masculine and feminine energy, individuals, teams, and organizations will realize fewer challenges and frustrations and enhanced success. Women work in companies, firms, universities, hospitals, major galleries, governments, and more. It's time to stop expecting them (and men) to leave major parts of themselves at home, especially when the talents and abilities we expect them to deny would benefit organizations.

WHAT DO WE DO NOW?

Inspired by the #MeToo movement and the Times Up activists, we can all act. We have spheres of influence. Your sphere of influence may only include yourself — okay. You might have a family at home, or you might lead a club in your neighborhood or church. Maybe you lead a team at work, or you're a C-suite executive or you sit on a couple of boards. Maybe you sit on your city council or you're a county commissioner. However large or small your sphere of influence is, you can take action. As Bob Dylan sang, "The times they are a-changin." They will change with or without you. I suggest you become part of the process for yourself and those you care about.

What is your sphere of influence? You control what you read, spend money on, watch on TV or the Internet, and what items you purchase. You influence through your relationships. Start making conscious choices today. Support women, the environment, feminist causes, family causes, and the arts. Support what feeds your feminine energy.

Take steps where you can. I believe in "toe in the water" approaches. When discussing intuition or a new hobby, take small steps at first. See how it goes. See how you feel. The more you enjoy your new behavior, the more you can ease forward. I liken this approach to easing into a body of water. Put your toe in first to test the water temperature. If it's fine, walk in to knee level. Then slowly walk into the water if it appeals to you. This differs from going from standing on dry land to diving into a body of water. With friends, family, and colleagues, you give them a chance to adjust to new aspects of you that you discover over time. And you can gauge reactions for your benefit as you change and explore your feminine energy. Please don't misunderstand me. You are not looking for others' approval. You are experimenting to see how YOU feel.

SOLUTIONS FOR INDIVIDUALS

Feminine energy gives us profound gifts that nurture and heal our souls and energize our spirits. We need time every day to feel, enjoy and grow our feminine energy. How do we do this? What will engage our feminine energy? Different habits work for different people. Try activities and see what seems right. Here are practices that my clients and I use to support personal feminine emergence:

Journaling – Writing for just a few minutes every day can help you get in touch with creative thoughts and with your emotions. Get yourself a special journal and make it private. Carve out time every day, ten to twelve minutes, and write your feelings and ideas, or write stream-of-consciousness thoughts. Write random thoughts that come to you. These may be from your intuition, your PGS. Pay attention to how you feel. More powerful and energizing thoughts hold more meaning for you. Reflect on those.

Meditating – I meditate every day. Beginners often find guided meditations useful. I recommend meditating every day for five minutes or more. You can find excellent guidelines on meditation in books or on the Internet. Find a place free of interruptions. Then relax, focus on your breathing, and clear your mind. Remember that if you are doing it, you are doing it right. Let perfectionism go. Let. It. Go. While following your breath, focus on one body part at a time (jaw, neck, shoulders, arms, back, etc.) and relax that area. I posted resources for meditation I like on my website under "Resources."

Challenge Beliefs – Challenge your beliefs about gender. Beliefs rule our worlds unconsciously. We learn our beliefs from our parents, who pass beliefs on to children unconsciously. It is our responsibility to challenge our beliefs as adults. Make sure your beliefs are constructive and that they work for you. If they are not, redesign your beliefs. Make sure you're living with positive beliefs about gender. See more information in Chapter 13.

Checking Emotions – Check in on your emotional state. Start by checking in once per hour. Set a timer to remind you. If it helps, put your hand over your heart. Attend to what you feel. Breathe, listen and observe sensations in your body. When we operate primarily in the masculine dimension, we focus on thoughts more than feelings. Your goal is to develop balance. By attending to feelings several times a day, we develop a skill we previously ignored or suppressed and make it a habit. Emotions provide guidance. We need to feel emotions and pay attention to them. It is not healthy to suppress or ignore our emotions.

Intuiting – Listen to your inner voice. We all have it. This is your Personal Guidance System. Do not ignore it or dismiss it. When you have a gut feeling or hear your inner voice, pause and attend to your senses. Process what your inner voice is saying. Do you feel excited? Do you feel warned? Start by following your intuition in small, safe ways. Build your confidence and your intuiting skills. You'll find resources for developing intuition on my website under "Resources."

Coaching – Working with a skilled coach on reconnecting with your feminine energy speeds up your ability to tap into and enjoy this vital Source. An experienced coach will give you resources and exercises that will stretch you at the right pace. Soon you will unconsciously align and integrate with feminine energy for a full, balanced, healthy and purposeful life. Today, thanks to the Internet, people engage coaches all over the world and meet via video chat. It's convenient, private, and fun. I highly recommend coaching.

SOLUTIONS FOR ORGANIZATIONS

When a group, team or organization is male-dominated, it is most likely dominated by masculine energy. Members of these teams or organizations describe them as "macho." This applies to societies and cultures as well. Leaders make a huge difference in defining the culture and tone of any group, team or organization. Leaders set expectations and also model what they expect. That is why it is so important for leaders to practice the solutions I have recommended for individuals. Leaders have the responsibility for optimizing the groups, teams, and organizations they lead. Their teams are only optimized if they are balanced. Leaders undermine their teams' success when they promote macho or masculine behaviors and cultures. Here are a few solutions that leaders can use to help balance their teams and support organizational feminine emergence:

Diversity – Leverage the diversity on your teams. Create diverse teams, and leverage masculine and feminine energies. Visibly reinforce and value feminine energies. Historically, we ignored, diminished, or negated these energies in the corporate world. If someone is a good listener, is collaborative, patient, or creative, acknowledge and reward those behaviors and skills. By acknowledging these skills in positive ways, you will help your employees realize you value feminine energies.

Team Building – Create team building events where feminine energies and behaviors or outcomes are openly recognized and rewarded. Create and complete activities where team members are rewarded for finding win-win solutions, working collaboratively, or taking a world or broad view. Provide times for team members to get to know each other personally and build relationships.

Your team members will develop trust and camaraderie that results in team performance and loyalty.

Challenge Beliefs – Challenge your team members' beliefs about gender. Each team member has unconscious beliefs about gender that they learned from their parents. We can challenge these beliefs as adults in fun and constructive ways through team building. Help your team members develop and sustain positive beliefs about gender. See more information in Chapter 13.

Intuition – When talking about an issue, ask team members if anyone has a gut feeling or intuitive sense that they would like to share. When someone shares an intuitive sense about a decision or an issue, explore that. Think through it a bit. Explore the possibilities of trusting it and moving forward. Take it seriously. Research shows that intuition can be effectively used for strategic decision-making in managerial decision making. This is notably true when managers with deep experience make rapid judgements regarding holistic associations (Dane and Pratt 2007).

Centering Rooms – A few companies have included centering rooms in their workplaces. They might call these meditation rooms, quiet rooms, or reflection spaces. It is a place for employees to go when they require solitude. An employee might need a moment to themselves because they perceive emotional reactions as inappropriate in the workplace. Crying and needing a moment alone are human experiences when dealing with challenging situations. I remember times of utter exhaustion and disappointment in my career when it was all I could do to make it to the furthest ladies' restroom in the building, hoping no other woman would be there, before I burst into tears. Even women can be heartless when someone is in pain. We want no one to see our sensitive side. We are all supposed to be so cold and robotic. A quiet place to think and process feelings can be a perfect solution. Afterward, employees return to work, focused and productive.

Win-Win Solutions – Look for win-win solutions. Make it a goal for everyone to walk away from conflict resolution feeling positive about the outcome. Expect team members to resolve negotiations, conflicts, and differences of opinion while maintaining or deepening relationships at the same time. Conflict resolution is an opportunity to maintain or enhance self-esteem of all parties. When working with feminine energy, conflicts become opportunities to build trust and deepen relationships.

Role Model – Show what you expect. Practice the solutions for individuals described earlier in this chapter and let your team members know you do. Share your feelings when they are relevant. Prioritize relationships at work and personally let your team members know you do. Prioritize your self-care and be an excellent listener. Your employees look to you as an example. They may or may not realize that they do, but they do. Set an example of balanced energy. They will follow your lead.

Consult – When you want to speed up the development of your team into a high-performing team and leverage all the energies — dormant and active — that your team possesses, work with a skilled and experienced consultant. A consultant will challenge you and your team at the right pace and in the right direction, so you get the balance and performance you desire.

MEN SUFFER TOO

I love men, I always have. I have never been a man hater. I love my husband, my dad, and my brother. I have worked with some extraordinary men, and have heterosexual and gay men in my life who I adore. I don't mind men having power as long as they handle it well. Handling it well, in part, means not being a bully. I don't like bullies, whether they are men or women, and I've known both. Having a balance of masculine and feminine energy, and having the balance that is right for you, is not about being male or female.

In the workplace, I have seen men perceived to be too feminine. They suffered negative consequences in their careers for being more sensitive or collaborative than others. Maybe they were good at building internal and external relationships. Regardless of their skills or tendencies, if decision makers perceived them as being too feminine, it hurt their careers. Whether these men were gay or straight was irrelevant. This consequence is shortsighted since good listeners, and collaborative individuals who focus on win-win solutions and building relationships, make excellent leaders. When men or women face these consequences, employees and organizations suffer, the bottom line suffers, and customers and stockholders suffer.

When organizations become too masculine, everyone suffers. I've known men who have suffered in those environments. They don't want to speak up because they know they would suffer consequences, just like women would. Years ago, I was teaching "Preventing Sexual Harassment" classes at a manufacturing company. After the class, there was a man, Fred, who waited until everyone exited so he could talk to me. Fred, a blue-collar worker in his fifties, had worked at the company for over twenty years. He said he wanted to thank me for teaching the class. Fred said it was very important to him. His value system included respect and dignity for everyone. He respected his wife and daughter and wanted others to as well.

At his work environment, Fred and his colleagues had lockers. Fred told me that a lot of his colleagues kept pornography in their lockers, which he found offensive. He said his colleagues knew how he felt, and they teased him. Fred hoped this training and the pertinent policies would change the culture and make it a better place to work. He hoped the stories and jokes men told on the night shift would stop because he did not like having to hear them. His story and gratitude touched me.

Fred worked in a hostile work environment due to an overly masculine, macho culture. If he'd spoken up, he would've made himself even more of an outcast and target in his work group. He stayed quiet and tried to be "one of the guys." I doubt he was alone. He and others suffered in this environment as so many have, and still do today. This is why we need change.

"

CAN YOU USE MORE PHYSICAL AND MENTAL ENERGY?
CAN YOUR TEAM USE MORE CREATIVITY?
DEVELOP HABITS THAT SUPPORT THE
FEMININE EMERGENCE OF YOU AND YOUR TEAM.
—Lisa Liszcz

12

Each Individual Needs Balance

CHAPTER 12

We all need balance, each one of us. Balance will look different for different people. Fred enjoyed more feminine energy in his life than some of his co-workers. During a few phases of my life, I enjoyed more masculine energy than feminine energy. When that lasted too long, I paid the price. Some of us thrive with more feminine energy in our lives, others thrive with more masculine energy. Still, others flourish with a perfect balance of feminine and masculine energies. I'm writing about individuals, but the same is true for groups and cultures. I'll explain with a few examples.

In 2015 my cat, Carbon, died. I had Carbon for sixteen of his seventeen years, he was my baby. He'd been sick on and off for two years, so his passing did not surprise me. While Carbon was sick, I said I would never have another pet. Pets are a hassle, they are expensive, you have to take them to the vet and buy them food, toys, and so on. You have to clean up after them, especially when they get sick.

I spent hundreds of dollars a month on Carbon near the end and got few full nights of sleep. Carbon took lots of medications and sub-cutaneous fluids. I gave him shots and pills, and I fed him human baby food. I was tired and emotionally drained at the end. I loved Carbon like my baby. I am a sensitive person. Somehow it is easier in our culture to be sensitive and emotional about animals than humans. The masculine makes that ok. We don't have to hide it too much. It can be "macho" to have a pet, an animal companion. I've always been connected to animals. Part of it for me is the intuition I feel for them. Most animals are intuitive, and I felt that with Carbon. Carbon would snuggle me when I was sad, and he would run around the house with bursts of energy when I was excited.

When Carbon died, I could hardly function. I missed him so much. For sixteen years he was my constant companion. He was with me through my divorce, my Ph.D. work, multiple home moves and job changes, being laid off, and the entire development of my relationship with my current husband, Michael, and our marriage. I loved Carbon deeply, and I missed him terribly. I needed to fill the deep hole in my heart. Even though I'd sworn to myself, "No more pets," when it came down to it, the divine feminine in me needed a fur baby to love, hold and take care of. I needed to nurture. I started looking online.

I wanted a small-to-medium size, fluffy companion dog. I browsed dog rescue websites. A few months earlier, my intuition told me to go to my friend, Barbara's, hairdresser, Tom, who had a Maltese named Belle that I fell madly in love with. While Tom styled my hair, I loved on Belle. Belle helped my recovery process after losing Carbon. Belle was a perfect size (about twelve pounds) and a wonderful companion dog. I read about the Maltese breed. Bred to be companion dogs, to be entertaining, loyal, loving, Maltese dogs sounded just like what I wanted. I loved Belle's big eyes and sweet, affectionate nature. I wanted a Maltese, I knew it in my heart. Meeting Belle was a gift the Universe gave me that I might have missed if I had not listened to my intuition. She helped me heal and sparked interest and direction in my feminine soul. I experienced simmerings of feminine emergence.

Looking for a Maltese online through adoption shelter websites, I found Penny. Her sweet face and those eyes took my breath away. I melted. Something clicked in my heart. She needed a mommy, and I was it. I knew it. Now I needed to tell Michael. Michael is sensitive and intuitive, and I love him so much for being very balanced. However, Michael is less into the non-physical than I am. I didn't trust that I could talk to him about my feelings of being guided by the divine feminine and my intuition.

I focused on objective details to start. I talked to him about us maybe having another pet (concrete conversation starter). I mentioned that we haven't had a dog together (fact-based and dichotomous point). I explained that a dog would help me walk more and help my back problems (fact and health-related data). I said that no cat would ever replace Carbon for us, I could not get another cat.

He asked me late on Thanksgiving evening, "Do you want to go meet her?"

My heart flipped. Could I possibly bring my baby home? Was I going to get the chance to love her? It seemed unfair for me to ask that we bring a new pet into the house. Pets are a lot of responsibility. We'd been through so much. And a puppy (Penny was sixteen weeks old) would be a tremendous responsibility. I operated as some unknown part of myself. Yes, I wanted her! I wanted her so much, but wanting her seemed crazy — even to me! I was the "No More Pets" lady. What was this new intensity, and where had my logical self gone?

We agreed to "meet" Penny. We drove to Conroe, Texas (about an hour's drive from our home) the Friday after Thanksgiving in 2015. It stormed on our drive, and Michael had a bad cold. We took Carbon's old cat carrier just in case we wound up bringing a puppy home (Michael's idea).

We walked into the pet adoption at Petco in Conroe, and I saw her right away. She was tiny, only about six pounds. Our eyes met, and I fell totally and completely in love. I loved everything about her. Her foster mom held her tightly. Penny looked around, wide-eyed. Foster Mommy asked me if I wanted to hold her. Hell yeah! I held her, and she cuddled me. Michael held her. She was sweet, clean, soft and precious. We put her on a leash and walked her around the store. You could tell she was curious and that her curiosity and timidity battled for control.

Foster Mommy asked us if we wanted to take her home. We said we needed to talk between the two of us for a bit. This was VERY spontaneous for us. We are two planners who are used to project plans, spreadsheets, and checklists. Within three days, we graduated from talking about possibly getting a dog to considering adopting one after a long drive on a rainy day. We felt giddy and crazy. We walked to the rear of Petco.

Michael started to barrage me with questions: "Do you think this is right? Do you think this really makes sense? Have you really thought this through? You've never had a dog, I have. Are you sure you want a dog? This dog?"

New to trusting Divine Guidance, I surprised myself when I said, "Could I have a minute?" For a millisecond, I wondered if that came out of someone else's mouth. He looked at me, wide-eyed, and said, "Yeah. Sure."

I walked around the store a bit. I quieted my mind. Once calmed and centered, I prayed, "Universe, God, Jesus, Divine Mother, if this is a good decision for me and Michael and Penny, please tell me."

I heard and felt the answer, "YES! GET THE DOG. TAKE HER HOME. LOVE HER. YES!" and I felt excited and happy, and I trusted this feeling. I. Trusted. This. Feeling. I took a radically new approach to decision-making, and I threw myself into my decision completely.

We told Foster Mommy that we would take Penny home with us that day. Foster Mommy generously showed us what type of food Penny ate, what type of bed she liked, and the type of chew toys she normally enjoyed. We loaded up our cart with goodies for Penny. We had not planned, so we did not have any puppy stuff at home. We needed everything.

Unlike us to be so spontaneous, it worked out great. Our adventure was fun, and I was so happy that I listened to my intuition. I'm so glad I asked the Universe for guidance. I'm so glad I embraced the part of myself that is mothering and nurturing and likes to cuddle and love and be loved. Penny looks at me so adoringly, still... over two years later. I thank God every day that she is in my life. She brings me, Michael, my step kids, neighbors, our dog walker, and so many others so much joy.

Our dog walker said to me, "Penny brings out the best in everyone." That is not entirely true. She can be a badass when she doesn't like someone or perceives someone (a dog, cat, squirrel, raccoon, a turned-over trash can, etc.) as a threat. She is tough, sweet, pretty, strong, playful, vicious, rascally, and smart. She is balanced. I love her so much. She has brought tremendous joy into our lives. I don't want to live without her. This is what happens when you open up to divine guidance and balance, and it is beautiful, exciting, and fun. If this is divine guidance and balance, count me in!

Maureen Murdock writes in her book *The Heroine's Journey* that women deny the feminine (Murdock 1990). We all deny the feminine. I was a "Feminine Denier," wearing boy shirts, ignoring my intuition and feelings, and acting tougher than I was. The feminine is not valued in our society. The cost we pay for that is tremendous and not sustainable.

We are killing our planet. We deny rights, skills, and natural talents of talented, insightful people in our society, missing out on valuable productivity and innovation. We kill joy and happiness and limit creativity and community. With heightened sensitivities in our culture now, how can we leverage new insights to move forward and embrace the feminine for balance? The answer is both individual and collective.

On an individual level, we need to embrace the characteristics of the feminine for more balance. We need to allow feminine energy to emerge. We can live consciously, embrace feminine characteristics and practice them ourselves. I've had to do this myself, being a recovering "Masculine Identifier" and "Feminine Denier."

When you see a feminine characteristic, instead of reacting automatically, pay attention to your heart's response. When I worked in corporate America, I worked at several companies where management looked down on professional women for becoming pregnant and taking maternity leave, or God forbid extended maternity leave. Management perceived a woman as "taking advantage of the system."

I am embarrassed now to say I agreed. I worked with a woman who was a Sr. Manager and one of the higher-level women employees where we worked. Within four years, she had three children. She took maternity leave three times. Managers saw this as an abuse of the maternity benefit; I did too. I harbored judgement towards her. It was easy to criticize, "Doesn't she know what causes that? Geez, she's popping out kids like a Pez dispenser! She's missing so much work!" Honestly, this characterized the company's "group think" of the "in-group."

The truth though was that she worked very hard and spent much of her maternity leave harboring guilt about missing work. Like many women, she worked while on maternity leave. I've had clients tell me how they exhaust themselves trying to be both super mom and super employee. The person who loses is the woman. She loses out on sleep, self-care, and time for restorative activities like hobbies and exercise. She usually puts herself last and is the one who pays the price while she takes care of everyone else's needs. Instead of admiring women for nurturing others AND taking care of demands at work, women are often criticized for never being enough. Having and raising children, being a dedicated and loving mother, and making sure children in our country experience love and care is a divine feminine responsibility.

Today, more men and women strive for balance. We can admire, support, and encourage the loving, nurturing aspects of parenting for ourselves and others. We can do this openly. Say to a friend, "I really admire how you are with your family," or, "I really admire that you put your kids first," or, "I admire how gentle you are with your kids, you are a great role model!" Tell a friend, "It is not easy to have balance. I see you doing your best, and I admire you."

Tell yourself the same. Journal to yourself that you are doing a good job and balance is a priority. Show respect for others who are exhibiting balance. Acknowledge them. Acknowledge yourself. Establish a pact with a friend or colleague to encourage each other concerning balance. Be real about it.

Explore your feelings of wanting to criticize the feminine when you see it. Where does this come from? Is it real? Does it serve you? Or does it come from a story that your parents or society fed you that does not serve you or the world anymore? When you find gaps in your thinking, and you want to explore an area of the feminine, think through alternatives to what your thinking has been.

For example, regarding the woman who gave birth to three children in four years, instead of thinking she took advantage of the company, I could have challenged that perception. I could have considered how special and miraculous it was that she had a beautiful family. I could examine where my beliefs came from and question their validity. I knew my colleague and knew that she had fertility issues for years. Her first child came with the help of fertility treatments. She and her husband conceived the next two babies naturally. What a miracle! Her family truly deserved to be celebrated. She was a loving mother and woman. She worked hard and was smart. She had the best intentions for the company and her family and worked circles around her male peers. Yet, people criticized her. I believe people resented her talent and masculine/feminine balance. Managers expected she would be masculine and out of balance. We worked in a male-dominated environment, and managers wanted her to be a little man. She was a woman, and she was absolutely lovely just as she was.

I have a therapist friend, a man, who talks to me about men adjusting to the changes in our culture. He works with men at his local fire department. He says there is so much pressure for the men to behave in a macho way, talking negatively about women, being pro-gun, excited about football, and generally bombastic and crude. Many of the men don't appreciate the culture, but they experience pressure to fit in. Many of the men's spouses work, so they are adjusting to things (laundry, cooking, cleaning, grocery shopping, etc.) not being done when they get home.

Men are STILL adjusting, even though substantial numbers of women have been in the workforce since the 1970s. That's fifty years - a generation. My friend tells me, and we see this in research studies, that men do not want to give up power. They perceive a letting go of power as a negative, and they believe they will not get anything of value in return. They can see embracing their feminine qualities as beneficial, yet they don't want to give up anything to get that benefit.

The men in this group understand that acts of nesting, caring for family, cooking food, and caring for one's personal items, such as clothes, can be rewarding and self-nurturing activities. Yet, they are conflicted. My friend told me that the men express interest in change and at the same time are fearful. We have decided in our culture that nurturing activities are feminine, and so they are devalued. This is key: we created those perceptions, and we can change them. We can shift our paradigms and live and enjoy the positive change. We can experience the joy in the opportunity to do these activities.

I recently talked with my personal coach about my life. We discussed joy, happiness, and energy. We talked about how feelings are choices. They are. We choose our emotions about everything. He asked when my emotions dip. I will preface this by saying that I have an amazing life. I have fought for it. I've taken risks and lived consciously, I am truly blessed with amazing relationships, the most amazing lover, partner, and friend in my husband, Michael, a beautiful home, and work that I love. And Penny.

When my coach asked when do my emotions dip, I said it's when I need to do laundry or grocery shopping. I said I hate doing chores, they are boring. He brilliantly said, "Are you kidding me? Really? Do you want some cheese with that whine?" and he and I both busted out laughing because he was right. Completely right.

For all my awareness and pride in my feminine energy, I caught myself not enjoying activities that our culture defines as "women's work." I let it bring me down. Then I chose differently. I chose to acknowledge it was a right and a privilege in this great country to go to one of our bright, clean, well-stocked grocery stores and shop for nutritious, tasty, beautiful food for me and my family. It is a privilege to care for the clothes that I love (I LOVE clothes!) that I've acquired locally and on travels over the years, unique pieces made by companies that share my values for gorgeous fabrics that lay luxuriously against my skin. It is a privilege.

One more chore I became tired of — and I'm ashamed to admit this — was walking Penny. I know in my heart, I am blessed to have the opportunity every day to take walks with that divine little furry spirit. I learn so much from her about curiosity, unconditional love, and boldness. I treasure my time with her.

After losing Carbon, I know I want to cherish every day that I get to love Penny. I choose to embrace every single day that I get to love Michael and all the special people in my life. I want to savor all the ways I get to love myself and all the ways I'm good to myself. I wish to do this in all ways possible. I want to embrace the feminine and masculine in myself to experience and share joy, love, and happiness. And if that means doing some laundry and grocery shopping, then I'm going to enjoy those activities too as nurturing, organic activities that enhance my life experience.

To live a balanced life is my opportunity and privilege as a human being. I want a full human experience. I wish to experience all of myself and life. I want to embrace all of it. I desire to be with others who embrace everything as well.

Together we will change the world.

"

GET ON THIS BEAUTIFUL FEMININE EMERGENCE BANDWAGON.
PUT A HALT ON DENYING THE FEMININE TODAY.
EMBRACE SWEET ASPECTS OF LIFE THAT MAKE YOU HAPPY,
AND LET'S MAKE THE WORLD A BETTER PLACE.
—Lisa Liszcz

Final Thoughts

CHAPTER 13

I'm not sure my mother hated me, but she never liked me. And she might have hated me. She did not want a girl. She never looked at me with love in her eyes, I never saw that look. I never saw her look at me as though she experienced delight to see me. She did not hug me and never told me she loved me. What I saw in her was contempt. That is what I invariably saw in her eyes.

Sometimes, we went years without speaking. When we were speaking, our conversations were one-sided. I listened to her complain about doctors, neighbors, and my father. I listened to her talk about the Kardashians or her daughter-in-law's family until I couldn't take it anymore, and then I'd end the conversation.

I go back to that she didn't want me. Because of that, I internalized her loathing. I believed I did not deserve love or to be wanted and adored. I shut down parts of my spirit for decades. At the same time, I internalized the loathing I had for her. I compounded the disdain she had for me being a girl with the disdain I felt for her weakness, vulnerability and femininity. I was determined to be nothing like her.

I wanted to prove that a woman could be everything a man could be - successful in the business world, independent, confident, bold and brave. I wanted to prove that I could earn enough money to support myself. I wanted to make it in a man's world. I thought maybe if I was enough like a man, she would love me. That did not work.

Because my mother kicked me out of the house, because she never loved me, and because she had such disdain for me, I pushed and pushed myself to succeed. I was alone from seventeen to twenty-six years old, so I had to be independent, I had to make my own way. No one gave me a safety net. No one told me, "There, there, Lisa. Everything will be okay." Until I was twenty-six, I only had myself to count on. I was born bold and became bolder. I worked in manufacturing companies, sat on all-male (except for me) leadership teams, led all-male teams of managers, and dressed like a little man. I made data-based decisions and was great at getting results. I embraced all my masculine energy and was rewarded for it.

These accomplishments came at a price. I felt empty and exhausted. I felt unappreciated. I felt I'd spent my life reaching for something special, achieving it, and finding it was not special at all. For decades, I diminished and disregarded the feminine in myself. I found companies and bosses who did the same. Only at the times in my life when I could embrace both masculine and feminine energies of myself and express my full, true self could I find joy and true fulfillment. Otherwise, life felt tough and draining.

Much of my life has been a reaction to my relationship with my mother. Living in this reaction mode overly stimulated the masculine energy in me and left the feminine energy to wither. When I started my first consulting company, I had a three-year period in my life when I rejuvenated my feminine energy. I thrived during that time. I developed and followed my intuition, leading me to an incredible relationship and a new marriage. I renewed my spiritual life and started journaling and meditating. But after I went back into the corporate world in 2004, my life grew out of balance again.

In time, I learned to appreciate who my mother was. In the last few years, I came to appreciate that much of who I am came from her. My love of beautiful things, lovely clothes, inviting spaces, my orientation in the non-physical and my emotional depth all come from my mother. I embrace these gifts from her now and am so very grateful to her for them. They are part of me, and engaging with and enjoying them adds quality and meaning to my life. I don't loathe or dismiss these aspects of myself or my life anymore. I embrace them. I prioritize them. This is part of my feminine emergence.

There is power in embracing gifts that are our birthright. Power. Most of my clients talk with me about self-esteem. We all need self-esteem. Women suffer from low self-esteem in the U.S. and around the world (Warrell 2018; Bleidorn et. al. 2016). We strengthen self-esteem when stepping into our power and embracing our God-given gifts. When we know who we are and embrace our true selves, we radiate that power.

I do. And I see it in others. This is not ego-driven power. This is the quiet, stealth power of the mama wolf. She knows what she needs to do and that she can and will do it. This is the power that comes from embracing the feminine energy within each of us.

"

WELCOME YOUR FEMININE EMERGENCE,
AND RADIATE POWER AND LOVE.
—Lisa Liszcz

Epilogue

CHAPTER 14

When you're a child, you trust everything your parents tell you. This is how we develop our beliefs. And our beliefs rule our world. As an adult, I've learned that my mother was right about some things, and she was wrong about other things.

She was wrong when she said, "Boys are better." That's simply not true.

She was right when she said, "It's a man's world." Yes, it is a white, heterosexual, horny, tall, protestant man's world, especially if he has good hair.

Here's the part she failed to add: It is also a Black man's world. It is a woman's world. It is a gay man's world, a lesbian's world, a transgender person's world, and a world for someone who is questioning, exploring, and figuring things out. It is a North American person's world, a Southern American person's world, a Middle Eastern person's world, a Far Eastern person's world, and so on. It is a world for every child, adult, and animal born on it. It is a world for everyone who is young and everyone who is old. It is a world for every permutation and combination of the demographics listed.

It is everyone's world. EVERYONE'S. Embrace that.

We are all responsible for questioning our beliefs as adults. As children, we learn things that don't serve us well as adults. We learn things from our parents that are simply not true, such as "Boys are better." Adults are responsible for managing the beliefs that unconsciously rule their world. Until we all challenge and rebuild our beliefs about gender, inequalities will continue. My mother did not mean to set her children up with misogynistic beliefs. She taught us what she had been taught, and she passed on her beliefs unconsciously. All parents do to some degree. As adults, it's our responsibility to break damaging cycles of belief.

I've made peace with my mother. She died on July 21, 2017. She never told me she loved me. At her death bed, I held her hand and sat with her. I told her, "Thank you for always showing me a strong woman. You were always strong."

I told her I loved her. She whispered with a fading breath, "Thank you."

I said, "I love you," and she said, "Thank you."

I repeated, "I love you," and she said, "Thank you."

We were looking into each other's eyes. She knew she was dying. In that incarnation, she just couldn't say it. And so it goes.

In my meditation life, I sometimes feel the energy of her soul. I hear her tell me she loves me and that we played our parts in the unfolding of the Universal Soul. She was tough on me, and I learned things from our relationship that give me perspective. And I'm not alone. I don't feel alone anymore. I plan to use what I've learned from my experience with my mother to help myself and others. I hope the dance she and I danced will move us all forward in The Great Unfolding.

One thing I've learned is that we don't always know why we go through what we go through. But we don't have to understand. We need to do our best. We need to listen to our soul's guidance and rise up to the highest ideals in our hearts. We are never alone. We are always guided. We need to listen and act with our soul guide. Sometimes our mother is our child, and our father is a fun friend, and we find parenting in people other than our parents. If we are lucky, we find good parenting deep within ourselves.

66

LET YOUR TRUE SELF TELL YOU WHAT TO BELIEVE.
NO ONE ELSE.
LET INTUITION GUIDE YOU.
LET YOUR FEMININE EMERGE.
—Lisa Liszcz

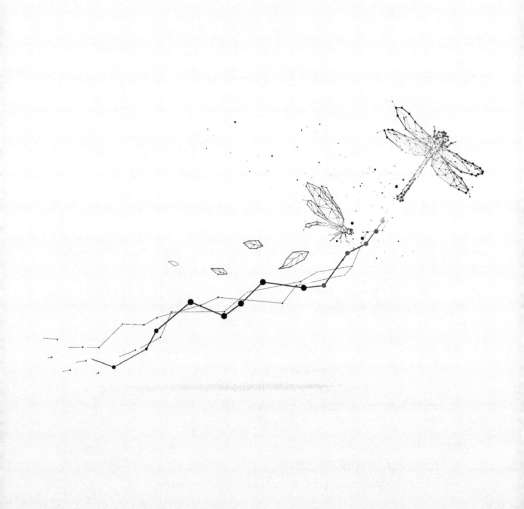

Bibliography

Achor, Shawn. *The Happiness Advantage: The Seven Principles of Positive Psychology That Fuel Success and Performance at Work.* 1st ed. New York: Broadway Books, 2010.

ACS. "Rosalyn Sussman Yalow (b. 1921) – American Chemical Society." *American Chemical Society.* Last modified June 21, 2013. https://www.acs.org/content/acs/en/education/whatischemistry/women-scientistsrosalyn-sussman-yalow.html.

Adams, Richard. "Female Graduates Find More Jobs, While Men Win Higher Pay." *The Guardian.* Last modified July 23, 2015. http://www.theguardian.com/education/2015/jul/23/women-graduates-find-more-jobs-while-men-win-higher-pay.

Alberts, Kate. "Fashion Flashback: The Evolution Of Menswear for Women." *Today Show.* Accessed January 14, 2018. https://www.today.com/style/fashion-flashback-menswear-style-celebrities-throughout-years-2D80457863.

Anderson, Mary. "Windshield Wipers." *Massachusetts Institute of Technology.* Accessed January 14, 2018. http://lemelson.mit.edu/resources/mary-anderson.

Barrett, Gena-mour. "How To Tell the Difference Between Me and the Only Other Black Girl Here." *Buzzfeed*. Accessed January 26, 2018. https://www.buzzfeed.com/genamourbarrett/how-to-tell-the-difference-between-me-and-the-other-black-gi.

Beauvoir, Simone de, Constance Borde, and Sheila Malovany-Chevallier. *The Second Sex*. London: Jonathan Cape, 2009.

Begley, Sarah. "Hillary Clinton Leads by 2.8 Million in Final Popular Vote Count." *TIME*. Accessed December 20, 2016. http://time.com/4608555/hillary-clinton-popular-vote-final/

Bellstrom, Kristen, and Beth Kowitt. "Check Out Fortune's 2017 Most Powerful Women in Business List." *Fortune*. Last modified September 21, 2017. http://fortune.com/most-powerful-women/.

Bem, Sandra Lipsitz. "Gender Schema Theory and Its Implications for Child Development: Raising Gender-Aschematic Children in a Gender-Schematic Society." *Journal of Women in Culture and Society* 8 (4) (1983):598-616.

Bennett, Bill. *PGS the Movie: Intuition is Your Personal Guidance System*. Sydney: B.J. Films distributed in the U.S. by GathrFilms, 2017.

Beyer, Kurt. *Grace Hopper and the Invention of the Information Age, Lemelson Center Studies In Invention and Innovation*. Cambridge: The MIT Press, 2009.

Bleidorn, W., R. C. Arslan, J. J. Denissen, P. J. Rentfrow, J. E. Gebauer, J. Potter, and S. D. Gosling. "Age and Gender Differences in Self-Esteem — A Cross-Cultural Window." *J Pers Soc Psychol* 111 (3)(2016):396-410. doi: 10.1037/pspp0000078.

Boatman, J., R. S. Wellins, and S. Neal. "Women Work: The Business Benefits of Closing the Gender Gap." *Global Leadership Forecast,* 2011.

Bradley, B. S., and S. K. Gobbart. "Determinants of Gender-Typed Play in Toddlers." *J Genet Psychol* 150 (4)(1989):453-5. doi:10.1080/0022 1325.1989.9914612.

Brehony, Kathleen A. *Awakening at Midlife: Realizing Your Potential for Growth and Change.* New York: Riverhead Books, 1996.

Bridges, Judith S. "Pink or Blue." *Psychology of Women Quarterly* 17(2) (2018):193-205. doi: 10.1111/j.1471-6402.1993.tb00444.x.

Calderone, Michael. "Anderson Cooper Bets Heavily That Stormy Is Serious News." *Politico.* Last modified March 25, 2018. https://politi.co/2ulEcas.

Casserly, Meghan. "The World's Most Powerful Female Entrepreneurs." *Forbes Media LLC.* Accessed January 14, 2018. https://www.forbes.com/pictures/lml45effkg/yang-lan-cofounder-sun-media/.

Catalyst. "Statistical Overview of Women in the Workforce." *Catalyst Inc.* Accessed January 16, 2018. http://www.catalyst.org/knowledge/statistical-overview-women-workforce.

Cooney, Samantha. "Here Are All the Public Figures Who've Been Accused of Sexual Misconduct After Harvey Weinstein." *TIME.* Accessed January 14, 2018. http://time.com/5015204/harvey-weinstein-scandal/.

Dane, Erik, and Michael G. Pratt. "Exploring Intuition and Its Role in Managerial Decision Making." *Academy of Management* 32 (1) (2007):33-54.

Digest of Education Statistics. "Table 318.30. Bachelor's, Master's, and Doctor's Degrees Conferred by Postsecondary Institutions, by Sex of Student and Discipline Division: 2014-15." *National Center for Education Statistics.* Accessed January 14, 2018. https://nces.ed.gov/programs/digest/d16/tables/dt16_318.30. asp?current=yes.

Downing, Nancy E., and Kristin L. Roush. "From Passive Acceptance to Active Commitment: A Model of Feminist Identity Development for Women." *The Counseling Psychologist* 13 (4)(1985):695-709.

Famous Women Inventors. "Stephanie Kwolek: Inventor of Kevlar®." Accessed January 14, 2018. http://www.women-inventors.com/Stephanie-Kwolek.asp.

Frankel, Lois P. *Nice Girls Don't Get the Corner Office: Unconscious Mistakes Women Make That Sabotage Their Careers.* Revised & updated first edition., A Nice Girls Book. New York: Business Plus, 2014.

Gilligan, Carol. *In a Different Voice: Psychological Theory and Women's Development.* Cambridge: Harvard University Press, 1993.

Goleman, Daniel, Richard E. Boyatzis, and Annie McKee. *Primal Leadership: Unleashing the Power of Emotional Intelligence.* Tenth anniversary edition. ed. Boston: Harvard Business Review Press, 2013.

Gray, Emma. "Why Anita Hill's 1991 Testimony is so Haunting Today." *HuffPost Women.* Last modified April 15, 2016. https://www.huffingtonpost.com/entry/anita-hill-matters-hbo-confirmation_us_570fb8f9e4b0ffa5937e5e72.

Gross, Kim Johnson, Jeff Stone, and Kristina Zimbalist. *Dress Smart — Women: Wardrobes That Win in the New Workplace,* Chic Simple. New York: Warner Books, 2002.

Heim, Pat, Tammy Hughes, and Susan K. Golant. *Hardball for Women: Winning at the Game of Business.* Revised & updated third edition. New York: Plume Book, 2015.

Helson, Ravenna. "Childhood Interest Clusters Related to Creativity in Women." *Journal of Consulting Psychology* 29 (4)(1965):352-361.

Helson, Ravenna. "A Longitudinal Study of Creative Personality in Women." *Creativity Research Journal* 12 (2)(2010):89-101.

Honig, Alice Sterling. "Sex Role Socialization in Early Childhood." *Young Children* 38 (6)(1983):57-70.

Hoogendoorn, Sander, Hessel Oosterbeek, and Mirja van Praag. "The Impact of Gender Diversity on the Performance of Business Teams: Evidence from a Field Experiment." *Management Science* 59 (7)(2013):1479-1724.

Izadi, Elahe. "Melissa Mccarthy Returns to SNL as an Even More Frustrated Sean Spicer." *The Washington Post.* Accessed January 14, 2018. https://www.washingtonpost.com/news/arts-and-entertainment/wp/2017/02/12/melissa-mccarthy-returns-to-snl-as-an-even-more-frustrated-sean-spicer/.

Jaffe, Kabir, and Ritama Davidson. *Indigo Adults: Understanding Who You Are and What You Can Become.* Franklin Lakes, NJ: New Page Books, 2009

Johnson, Allan G. *The Blackwell Dictionary of Sociology: A User's Guide to Sociological Language.* 2nd ed. Oxford, England; Malden, MA: Blackwell Publishers, 2000.

Kyle, Kim, Christina Littlefield, and Melissa Etehad. "Bill Cosby: A 50-Year Chronicle of Accusations and Accomplishments." *Los Angeles Times*. Accessed January 15, 2018. http://www.latimes.com/entertainment/la-et-bill-cosby-timeline-htmlstory.html.

Langone, Alix. "#Metoo and Time's Up Founders Explain the Difference Between the 2 Movements." *TIME*. Last modified March 22, 2018. http://time.com/5189945/whats-the-difference-between-the-metoo-and-times-up-movements/

LearnAboutNature.com. "How Long Do Dragonflies Live?" Accessed September 20, 2018. https://www.dragonfly-site.com/how-long-dragonflies-live.html

LeBlanc, Gabrielle. "5 Things Happy People Do." *OWNTV*. Accessed January 22, 2018. http://www.oprah.com/spirit/5-things-every-happy-woman-does.

Lester-Coll, Gabby. "Men Are From Mars, Women Are From Venus: Masculine Vs. Feminine Energy." *The S Life Mag*. Accessed January 20, 2018. https://www.sakara.com/blogs/mag/115704133-men-are-from-mars-women-are-from-venus-masculine-vs-feminine-energy.

Leyens, Jacques–Philippe, Armando Rodriguez–Perez, Ramon Rodriguez–Torres, Ruth Gaunt, Maria–Paola Paladino, Jeroen Vaes, and Stéphanie Demoulin. "Psychological Essentialism and the Differential Attribution of Uniquely Human Emotions to Ingroups and Outgroups." *European Journal of Social Psychology* 31(4)(2001):395-411. https://onlinelibrary.wiley.com/doi/abs/10.1002/ejsp.50

Lindqvist, Erik. "Height and Leadership." *The Review of Economics and Statistics* 94 (4)(2012):1191-1196.

Little, Julia. "Frailty Thy Name is Woman: Depictions of Female Madness." *MFA, Dramatic Literature, Criticism and Theory Commons*, Virginia Commonwealth University, 2015.

Los Angeles Times. "Bill Cosby Sex Assault Allegations and Charges – LA Times." Accessed January 14, 2018. http://www.latimes.com/entertainment/tv/la-et-st-bill-cosby-allegations-sg-storygallery.html.

Merriam-Webster Inc. *The Merriam-Webster Dictionary.* New edition. Springfield, Massachusetts: Merriam-Webster, Incorporated, 2016

Molloy, John T. *New Women's Dress for Success.* New York: Warner Books, 1996.

Movemeon. "Women are One Third More Likely to Get Hired Than Men." *Insight.* Last modified May 15, 2017. http://insight.movemeon.com/insight-analysis/gender/women-more-likely-to-get-hired-than-men.

Murdock, Maureen. *The Heroine's Journey.* 1st ed. New York: Shambhala; Distributed in the U.S. by Random House, 1990.

Norman, Matthew. "Stormy Daniels is Emerging as the Feminist Hero from the Donald Trump Affair." *Independent.* Last modified March 25, 2018. https://www.independent.co.uk/voices/stormy-daniels-donald-trump-affair-cbs-interview-latest-michael-cohen-a8273126.html.

Petersen, Anne Helen. *Too Fat, Too Slutty, Too Loud: The Rise and Reign of the Unruly Woman.* New York: Plume, 2017.

Pianin, Eric. 2017. "Data Shows Millennial Women are Dominating the Current Job Market." *Inc.* Last modified May 23, 2017.

https://www.inc.com/the-fiscal-times/millennial-women-dominate-job-market-men-overshadowed.html.

Pogrebin, Robin. 2018. "Peter Martins Retires from New York City Ballet after Misconduct Allegations." *The New York Times Company*. Last modified January 1, 2018.
https://www.nytimes.com/2018/01/01/arts/dance/peter-martins-resigns-ballet.html.

Roberts, Roxanne. "'It Was Just Awful': The Clarence Thomas Hearings, in the Words of Those Who were There." *The Washington Post*, 2016. Accessed January 10, 2018.
https://www.washingtonpost.com/lifestyle/style/it-was-just-awful-the-clarence-thomas-hearings-in-the-words-of-those-who-were-there/2016/04/07/662eda1a-f120-11e5-85a6-2132cf446d0a_story.html.

Rothfeld, Michael, and Joe Palazzolo. "Trump Lawyer Arranged $130,000 Payment for Adult-Film Star's Silence." *The Wall Street Journal*. Last modified January 12, 2018.

Sage, Purple. "What it Means to be 'Woman-Identified' or 'Male-Identified'." *Purple Sage*, March 29, 2015. Accessed January 14, 2018.
https://purplesagefem.wordpress.com/2015/03/29/what-it-means-to-be-woman-identified-or-male-identified/.

Schwantes, Marcel. "10 Compelling Reasons Servant Leadership May be the Best, Says Science." *Inc*. Accessed January 16, 2018.
https://www.inc.com/marcel-schwantes/10-convincing-reasons-to-consider-servant-leadership-according-to-research.html.

Shetterly, Margot Lee. *Hidden Figures: The Untold True Story of Four African-American Women Who Helped Launch Our Nation Into Space*. Young Readers' Edition. London: Harper Collins, 2016

Steel, Emily, and Michael S. Schmidt. "Bill O'Reilly Settled New Harassment
    Claim, Then Fox Renewed His Contract." *The New York Times
    Company*. Last modified October 21, 2017.
    https://www.nytimes.com/2017/10/21/business/media/bill-oreilly-
    sexual-harassment.html.

Stulp, Gert, Abraham P. Buunk, Simon Verhulst, and Thomas V. Pollet. "Tall
    Claims? Sense and Nonsense about the Importance of Height of US
    Presidents." *The Leadership Quarterly* 24 (1)(2013):159-171. doi:
    https:// doi.org/10.1016/j.leaqua.2012.09.002.

Suro, Robert. "The Thomas Nomination: A Law Professor Defends Integrity."
    The New York Times. Last modified August 8, 1991.
    http://www.nytimes.com/1991/10/08/us/the-thomas-nomination-a-
    law-professor-defends-integrity.html.

Tajfel, Henri. "Experiments in Intergroup Discrimination." *Scientific American*
    223 (5)(1970):96-103.

Thaves, Bob. Frank and Ernest: *Batteries Not Included*. New York: Holt,
    Rinehart, and Winston, 1983.

The Editors of Time Magazine. "46 Women Who are Changing the World."
    TIME. Accessed January16, 2018.
    http://time.com/collection/firsts/.

United States Department of Labor. "Women at Work: Spotlight on Statistics."
    U.S. Bureau of Labor Statistics. Accessed January 14, 2018.
    https://www.bls.gov/spotlight/2017/women-at-work/home.htm.

Warrell, Margie. "For Women to Rise We Must Close 'The Confidence Gap'." *Forbes Media LLC.* Accessed January 20, 2018. https://www.forbes.com/sites/margiewarrell/2016/01/20/gender-confidence-gap/. Wikipedia. "Ursula Burns."

Wikipedia. "Ursula Burns." *Wikipedia.* Last modified August 15, 2017. https://en.wikipedia.org/wiki/Ursula_Burns.

Wolf, Naomi. *The Beauty Myth: How Images of Beauty are Used Against Women.* New York: Perennial, 2002.

Worthen, Meredith. "Celebrating America's First Women CEOs." *Biography.com.* Last modified January 20, 2016. https://www.biography.com/news/first-female-ceos-in-history.

Yonack, Lyn. "Sexual Assault is About Power." *PsychologyToday.* Accessed November 14, 2017. https://www.psychologytoday.com/blog/psychoanalysis-unplugged/201711/sexual-assault-is-about-power.

Zachary, Stephanie, Eliana Dockterman, and Haley Sweetland Edwards. "TIME Person of the Year 2017: The Silence Breakers." *TIME.* Accessed January 21, 2018. http://time.com/time-person-of-the-year-2017-silence-breakers/.

with love,
Lisa

www.FeminineEmergence.love

CPSIA information can be obtained
at www.ICGtesting.com
Printed in the USA
LVHW041110191118
597620LV00015B/349/P